Joyce Appleby on *Thomas Jefferson*
Louis Auchincloss on *Theodore Roosevelt*
Jean H. Baker on *James Buchanan*
H. W. Brands on *Woodrow Wilson*
Alan Brinkley on *John F. Kennedy*
Douglas Brinkley on *Gerald R. Ford*
Josiah Bunting III on *Ulysses S. Grant*
James MacGregor Burns and Susan Dunn on *George Washington*
Charles W. Calhoun on *Benjamin Harrison*
Gail Collins on *William Henry Harrison*
Robert Dallek on *Harry S. Truman*
John W. Dean on *Warren G. Harding*
John Patrick Diggins on *John Adams*
Elizabeth Drew on *Richard M. Nixon*
John S. D. Eisenhower on *Zachary Taylor*
Paul Finkelman on *Millard Fillmore*
Annette Gordon-Reed on *Andrew Johnson*
Henry F. Graff on *Grover Cleveland*
David Greenberg on *Calvin Coolidge*
Gary Hart on *James Monroe*
Michael F. Holt on *Franklin Pierce*
Roy Jenkins on *Franklin Delano Roosevelt*
Zachary Karabell on *Chester Alan Arthur*
William E. Leuchtenburg on *Herbert Hoover*
James Mann on *George W. Bush*
Gary May on *John Tyler*
George McGovern on *Abraham Lincoln*
Timothy Naftali on *George H. W. Bush*
Charles Peters on *Lyndon B. Johnson*
Kevin Phillips on *William McKinley*
Robert V. Remini on *John Quincy Adams*
Jeffrey Rosen on *William Howard Taft*
Ira Rutkow on *James A. Garfield*
John Seigenthaler on *James K. Polk*
Michael Tomasky on *Bill Clinton*
Hans L. Trefousse on *Rutherford B. Hayes*
Jacob Weisberg on *Ronald Reagan*
Tom Wicker on *Dwight D. Eisenhower*
Ted Widmer on *Martin Van Buren*
Sean Wilentz on *Andrew Jackson*
Garry Wills on *James Madison*
Julian E. Zelizer on *Jimmy Carter*

William Howard Taft

Jeffrey Rosen

William
Howard Taft

THE AMERICAN PRESIDENTS

ARTHUR M. SCHLESINGER, JR., AND SEAN WILENTZ

GENERAL EDITORS

Times Books

HENRY HOLT AND COMPANY, NEW YORK

Times Books
Henry Holt and Company
Publishers since 1866
175 Fifth Avenue
New York, New York 10010
www.henryholt.com

Henry Holt® is a registered trademark of
Macmillan Publishing group, LLC.

Frontispiece: Library of Congress, LC-USZ62-96924

Library of Congress Cataloging-in-Publication Data

Names: Rosen, Jeffrey, 1964– author.
Title: William Howard Taft : the 27th president, 1909–1913 / Jeffrey Rosen.
Description: First edition. | New York : Henry Holt and Company, 2018. |
    Series: The American presidents series | Includes bibliographical references
    and index.
Identifiers: LCCN 2017048466 | ISBN 9780805069549 (hardcover : alk. paper)
Subjects: LCSH: Taft, William H. (William Howard), 1857–1930. | Presidents—
    United States—Biography. | United States—Politics and government—1909–1913.
Classification: LCC E762 .R58 2018 | DDC 973.912092 [B]—dc23
LC record available at https://lccn.loc.gov/2017048466

Our books may be purchased in bulk for promotional, educational, or business
use. Please contact your local bookseller or the Macmillan Corporate and
Premium Sales Department at (800) 221-7945, extension 5442, or by e-mail at
MacmillanSpecialMarkets@macmillan.com.

First Edition 2018

Printed in the United States of America

3   5   7   9   10   8   6   4   2

For Lauren Coyle Rosen

More than I ever had hoped, what happiness I have been granted!
Love led me wisely through Rome, passing its palaces by.
—Goethe, *Roman Elegies*

Contents

Editor's Note

THE AMERICAN PRESIDENCY

The president is the central player in the American political order. That would seem to contradict the intentions of the Founding Fathers. Remembering the horrid example of the British monarchy, they invented a separation of powers in order, as Justice Brandeis later put it, "to preclude the exercise of arbitrary power." Accordingly, they divided the government into three allegedly equal and coordinate branches—the executive, the legislative, and the judiciary.

But a system based on the tripartite separation of powers has an inherent tendency toward inertia and stalemate. One of the three branches must take the initiative if the system is to move. The executive branch alone is structurally capable of taking that initiative. The Founders must have sensed this when they accepted Alexander Hamilton's proposition in the Seventieth Federalist that "energy in the executive is a leading character in the definition of good government." They thus envisaged a strong president—but within an equally strong system of constitutional accountability. (The term *imperial presidency* arose in the 1970s to describe the situation when the balance between power and accountability is upset in favor of the executive.)

The American system of self-government thus comes to focus in the presidency—"the vital place of action in the system," as Woodrow Wilson put it. Henry Adams, himself the great-grandson and grandson of presidents as well as the most brilliant of American historians, said that the American president "resembles the commander of a ship at sea. He must have a helm to grasp, a course to steer, a port to seek." The men in the White House (thus far only men, alas) in steering their chosen courses have shaped our destiny as a nation.

Biography offers an easy education in American history, rendering the past more human, more vivid, more intimate, more accessible, more connected to ourselves. Biography reminds us that presidents are not supermen. They are human beings too, worrying about decisions, attending to wives and children, juggling balls in the air, and putting on their pants one leg at a time. Indeed, as Emerson contended, "There is properly no history; only biography."

Presidents serve us as inspirations, and they also serve us as warnings. They provide bad examples as well as good. The nation, the Supreme Court has said, has "no right to expect that it will always have wise and humane rulers, sincerely attached to the principles of the Constitution. Wicked men, ambitious of power, with hatred of liberty and contempt of law, may fill the place once occupied by Washington and Lincoln."

The men in the White House express the ideals and the values, the frailties and the flaws, of the voters who send them there. It is altogether natural that we should want to know more about the virtues and the vices of the fellows we have elected to govern us. As we know more about them, we will know more about ourselves. The French political philosopher Joseph de Maistre said, "Every nation has the government it deserves."

At the start of the twenty-first century, forty-two men have made it to the Oval Office. (George W. Bush is counted our forty-third president, because Grover Cleveland, who served nonconsecutive terms, is counted twice.) Of the parade of presidents, a dozen or so lead the polls periodically conducted by historians and political scientists. What makes a great president?

Great presidents possess, or are possessed by, a vision of an ideal America. Their passion, as they grasp the helm, is to set the ship of state on the right course toward the port they seek. Great presidents also have a deep psychic connection with the needs, anxieties, dreams of people. "I do not believe," said Wilson, "that any man can lead who does not act . . . under the impulse of a profound sympathy with those whom he leads—a sympathy which is insight—an insight which is of the heart rather than of the intellect."

"All of our great presidents," said Franklin D. Roosevelt, "were leaders of thought at a time when certain ideas in the life of the nation had to be clarified." So Washington incarnated the idea of federal union, Jefferson and Jackson the idea of democracy, Lincoln union and freedom, Cleveland rugged honesty. Theodore Roosevelt and Wilson, said FDR, were both "moral leaders, each in his own way and his own time, who used the presidency as a pulpit."

To succeed, presidents not only must have a port to seek but they must convince Congress and the electorate that it is a port worth seeking. Politics in a democracy is ultimately an educational process, an adventure in persuasion and consent. Every president stands in Theodore Roosevelt's bully pulpit.

The greatest presidents in the scholars' rankings, Washington, Lincoln, and Franklin Roosevelt, were leaders who confronted and overcame the republic's greatest crises. Crisis widens presidential opportunities for bold and imaginative action. But it does not guarantee presidential greatness. The crisis of secession did not spur Buchanan or the crisis of depression spur Hoover to creative leadership. Their inadequacies in the face of crisis allowed Lincoln and the second Roosevelt to show the difference individuals make to history. Still, even in the absence of first-order crisis, forceful and persuasive presidents—Jefferson, Jackson, James K. Polk, Theodore Roosevelt, Harry Truman, John F. Kennedy, Ronald Reagan, George W. Bush—are able to impose their own priorities on the country.

The diverse drama of the presidency offers a fascinating set of tales. Biographies of American presidents constitute a chronicle of wisdom and folly, nobility and pettiness, courage and cunning, forthrightness and deceit, quarrel and consensus. The turmoil perennially swirling around the White House illuminates the heart of the American democracy.

It is the aim of the American Presidents series to present the grand panorama of our chief executives in volumes compact enough for the busy reader, lucid enough for the student, authoritative enough for the scholar. Each volume offers a distillation of character and career. I hope that these lives will give readers some understanding of the pitfalls and potentialities of the presidency and also of the responsibilities of citizenship. Truman's famous sign—"The buck stops here"—tells only half the story. Citizens cannot escape the ultimate responsibility. It is in the voting booth, not on the presidential desk, that the buck finally stops.

—Arthur M. Schlesinger, Jr.

William Howard Taft

Introduction

Judicial President and
Presidential Chief Justice

In 1905, as secretary of war, William Howard Taft set out on a diplomatic mission to the Far East. Stopping off at the Imperial Palace in Tokyo, Taft received from the empress of Japan an elaborate tapestry for his wife, Nellie, a copy from the Gobelin original, showing the meeting of Columbus and Isabella. When Taft brought the gift home, Nellie protested that it was too large to be of use. "Oh well, never mind," Taft declared. "I'm going to present it to the Smithsonian Institute anyway, because you know, my dear, it is against the Constitution for an official in the United States government to accept any kind of favours from foreign courts." Nellie had often "met the Constitution face to face," she recalled, but had previously accepted "its decrees with what I had hoped was patriotic resignation." This time, however, she changed her mind. Nellie decided she wanted to keep the tapestry after all.[1]

Mrs. Taft then tried to persuade her husband, a former judge, that she was not an official of the United States government and therefore was not bound by the foreign emoluments clause of the Constitution. Taft "stood firmly by the Constitution, as usual," Nellie recalled with bemused exasperation, "and eventually I had to submit the question for arbitration to President Roosevelt, who agreed with me that I was a private citizen and had a perfect right to accept the gift." After Taft became president, she hung the tapestry in the state dining room of the White House, where she took pleasure in watching guests attempt in vain to decipher its meaning.[2]

Nellie Taft's verdict about her husband's judicial scruples—"he stood firmly by the Constitution, as usual"—serves as a fitting epitaph for his entire career. William Howard Taft, the only president who went on to serve as chief justice of the United States, devoted his leadership of the executive and judicial branches to defending the U.S. Constitution above all. Earlier in his career, Taft had served as solicitor general in the U.S. Department of Justice, representing the United States before the Supreme Court. The experience quickened his judicial ambitions. His next appointment was to the U.S. Court of Appeals for the Sixth Circuit, which he found a kind of heaven; after eight years, President William McKinley persuaded him to resign to become governor-general of the Philippines, another appointment that delighted him because it cast him as Solon, a constitution maker applauded by a grateful people. He declined President Theodore Roosevelt's repeated offers of a Supreme Court seat with the greatest reluctance and agreed instead to serve as secretary of war, a position once held by his revered father, where he endeared himself to the president for his deference and administrative efficiency. Yearning as always for the bench, he was persuaded by his wife to run for president in 1908, and his victory fulfilled her ambition while thwarting his own.

In the White House, Taft approached the presidency not as a politician but as a judge. He pledged to put Roosevelt's policies, many of them enacted by executive order, on firm constitutional grounds by persuading Congress to endorse them. And he approached each presidential decision by asking whether it comported with the Constitution. Unlike Roosevelt, who declared that a president could do anything the Constitution didn't forbid, Taft insisted that he could do only what the Constitution explicitly allowed. This caused a dramatic breach with Roosevelt, leading to the historic election of 1912, which Taft viewed as a crusade to defend the Constitution against what he considered the demagogic populism of Roosevelt and Woodrow Wilson. The people disagreed, and Taft was defeated.

Nine years later, Taft fulfilled his lifelong dream when President Warren Harding appointed him chief justice. And he achieved on the Court many of the remaining constitutional goals he had set for himself as president, promoting consensus among the justices and establishing the federal judiciary as a modern, strong, and fully equal branch of government, ready to defend constitutional rights and liberties against the encroachments of the political branches and against new populist threats. To emphasize the independence of the judicial branch, he oversaw the construction of a new Supreme Court building, which allowed the Court to move from its cramped headquarters in the basement of the Capitol to a majestic Temple of Justice across the street. If Taft had chafed in the White House as a judicial president, he thrived on the Supreme Court as a presidential chief justice.

Taft is remembered today as an average president, and most ratings of presidential historians place him in the middle. The 2017 C-SPAN Presidential Historians Survey, for example, ranks Taft overall at twenty-fourth—just below Ulysses S. Grant and Grover Cleveland, but substantially below his rivals in the election of 1912, Theodore Roosevelt and Woodrow Wilson, who rank fourth and eleventh, respectively.[3] As chief justice, by contrast, Taft ranks much higher. A 1993 survey of judicial historians ranked him fifth among the sixteen chief justices who had served to that date, trailing only John Marshall, Earl Warren, Charles Evans Hughes, and Harlan Fiske Stone.[4]

When Taft's constitutional achievements as president and chief justice are viewed of a piece, his significance comes into proper focus. As Judge Douglas Ginsburg of the U.S. Court of Appeals for the D.C. Circuit told me, "William Howard Taft is the most underappreciated constitutional figure since George Mason, who refused to sign the original Constitution because it didn't have a Bill of Rights." As judge, colonial governor, cabinet secretary, president, and chief justice, Taft had a clear and consistent constitutional vision, and he achieved nearly all of the constitutional goals he set for himself, even if as a politician he often fell short. A disciple of John Marshall and the authors of the *Federalist Papers*—James Madison, Alexander Hamilton, and John Jay— Taft believed that the presidency, the Congress, and the judiciary should be strong and independent branches, each exercising broad but limited powers within clearly defined constitutional boundaries. And he insisted that constitutional filters on the direct expression of popular passion were necessary to promote the "wise deliberation . . . which may constitute the salvation of the Republic."[5] Without these filters, he feared, America would degenerate from a representative republic into a direct democracy, and populist demagogues would flatter the people into subverting the constitutional order.

This short book offers an interpretation of William Howard Taft's presidency as he himself understood it: in constitutional rather than political terms. There are many fine political biographies of Taft, and many reach an ambivalent verdict. Henry Pringle, Taft's first biographer, wrote of his subject in 1939 with stylish condescension, concluding accurately but waspishly that Taft "had a thorough mind rather than a facile or brilliant one" and that his judicial opinions, like his letters and presidential speeches, were "too verbose and rarely had charm."[6] Twenty-five years later, Alpheus Mason, in the most comprehensive study of Taft's Supreme Court career, began by noting:

> For Americans of my generation, the conventional image
> of William Howard Taft is unflattering. It pictures him as

a stubborn defender of the status quo, champion of property rights, apologist for privilege, inveterate critic of social democracy—the gigantic symbol of standpattism. Weighing well over three hundred pounds, avoirdupois alone made him a cartoonist's model of the bloated capitalist or political boss.[7]

Mason does not entirely dispel this caricature.

More recent studies—including superb books by Judith Anderson (on Taft's psychology and character), David H. Burton (on his foreign policy), Doris Kearns Goodwin (on his relationship with Theodore Roosevelt and the press), Lewis L. Gould (on his presidency), and Jonathan Lurie (on his progressive conservatism)—view Taft as a man of rectitude who lacked political skills. "Widely admired in his day for his integrity and strong sense of morality," Lurie writes, "Taft seems to have set a standard for personal conduct that later presidents have had, to put it mildly, some difficulty in attaining."[8] These biographers recognize that Taft had a judicial temperament that was ill equipped for the political demands of the twentieth-century presidency. But they take him to task for refusing to engage in popular leadership—precisely the kind of leadership that Taft's constitutional vision of the presidency forbade.

Taft, however, was unapologetic about his embrace of a constitutional rather than a popular conception of the presidency. "I will not play a part for popularity," he told his military aide Archie Butt, who served and admired both Roosevelt and Taft and whose letters provide the most intimate and balanced contemporary account of Taft's presidency and character. "If the people do not approve of me or of my administration after they have had time to know me, then I shall not let it worry me, and I most certainly shall not change my methods."[9] And Taft was more successful in achieving his goals than many observers have recognized. He extended federal environmental protection to more land than Roosevelt and brought more antitrust suits in one term than Roosevelt brought in nearly two. Slashing federal expenses, he turned a budget deficit of $89 million in 1909 into a budget surplus of $11 million in 1911. As a moderate free trader, he passed the first reduction in the federal tariff since the 1890s, a political third rail Roosevelt had avoided. He persuaded Congress to pass a landmark Canadian free trade agreement (although Canadian voters ultimately rejected it), and he maintained peace with Mexico by refusing to send troops over the border despite cries in his own party to start a war. He defended judicial independence against the demagogic attacks of Roosevelt, who assailed individual judges by name and sought to overturn judicial decisions by popular vote.

Throughout his career, Taft's abiding goal was to perfect the administration of what he called "the machinery of government with a view to increasing its efficiency and decreasing its cost."[10] Henry Stimson, who served as secretary of war under Presidents Taft, Franklin Roosevelt, and Harry Truman, and as secretary of state under Herbert Hoover, said that Taft was the finest administrator of them all.[11] Taft's talent for administration allowed him to fulfill his campaign promise to oversee a government that was constitutionally limited and economically efficient. And as chief justice, Taft deployed his gifts as an administrator and mediator to achieve many of his remaining goals, reforming the federal rules of judicial procedure and establishing the federal judiciary as a strong and independent branch of government, ready to check the excesses of the political branches in the face of new populist threats.

For all Taft's judicial virtues—his devotion to constitutional limitations, his scrupulous honesty, his skill as an administrator, and his respect for the prerogatives of Congress and the courts— he cannot be considered an entirely successful president, because successful presidents need to exercise the popular leadership Taft disdained. Instead of trying to persuade Congress to adopt his proposed tariff reform, for example, Taft simply sent a 340-word legalistic message and left it at that, because he believed the Constitution allowed the president to recommend laws but not to lobby for them. (As chief justice, he took a different view of lobbying for judicial reform.) Devoted to party unity above all, Taft put too much trust in the Republican leaders known as "standpat conservatives," led by Speaker Joe Cannon, who watered down his proposed tariff reforms and refused to endorse the international courts that he considered necessary for global peace. Moreover, because of his thin-skinned sensitivity to criticism, Taft impetuously fired those he considered disloyal, with disastrous political consequences, culminating in his rift with Theodore Roosevelt and the fracturing of the Republican Party.

Still, it is important to understand Taft's refusal to exert popular leadership as part of his constitutional conception of the presidency. Like the Framers, Taft saw the president's role as that of a kind of chief magistrate who would promote thoughtful deliberation among the people's representatives without directly representing the people's momentary passions. Seen in this light, Taft's political vice was a constitutional virtue, better suited to the bench than to the White House, no doubt, but based on principle and not personality.

Taft's principles, in turn, led to his rift with Roosevelt, which continues to define our modern debates over the constitutional powers of the president. "The thing which impresses me most is not the power I have to exercise under the Constitution, but the limitations and restrictions to which I am subject under that instrument,"[12] Taft declared in 1909, a year after his election as president. Taft was appalled, therefore, the following year, when Theodore Roosevelt delivered his famous "New Nationalism" speech in Osawatomie, Kansas, in which Roosevelt declared, "This New Nationalism regards the executive power as the steward of the public welfare." In his autobiography, published in 1913, Roosevelt elaborated on his view: "My belief was that it was not only [the president's] right but his duty to do anything that the needs of the Nation demanded unless such action was forbidden by the Constitution or by the laws." As he dramatically concluded, "I did not usurp power, but I did greatly broaden the use of executive power."[13]

Taft strongly disagreed with Roosevelt's "stewardship" vision. "The true view of the Executive functions is, as I conceive it, that the President can exercise no power which cannot be fairly and reasonably traced to some specific grant of power," Taft wrote in *Our Chief Magistrate and His Powers*, published in 1916. Anticipating the position of strict constructionist Republicans today, Taft continued, "Such specific grant must be either in the Federal Constitution or in an act of Congress passed in pursuance thereof."[14] Taft was similarly appalled by Roosevelt's populist attacks on judges—in particular, by his proposal to allow Americans to overturn judicial decisions by popular vote—and he decided that the central question in the election of 1912 was judicial independence.

Taft viewed the election of 1912 as a choice between the Founders' conception of the presidency as a constrained office, defined and limited by the Constitution, and the views of his progressive rivals Theodore Roosevelt and Woodrow Wilson, who, in different ways, viewed the presidency as a popular office, directly accountable to the people. While Roosevelt saw the president as a "steward" of the people, Wilson criticized the separation of powers and natural rights as an eighteenth-century anachronism, insisting that the twentieth century demanded a large, energetic federal government overseen by a president directly responsive to the people's will.[15] Taft, like the Founders, rejected the idea of popular leadership by the president, but Roosevelt and Wilson insisted on it. For Taft, the president's authority came from the Constitution; for Roosevelt and Wilson, it came directly from the people. Although Roosevelt and Wilson believed in rule by experts who were accountable to the president, they championed reforms like the initiative, referendum, and direct primary that would limit the ability of representatives and independent judges to filter popular passions. They also criticized judges for checking progressive legislation and thwarting the immediate expression of the people's will.

Taft, by contrast, insisted that the Founders intended to create a republic rather than a pure democracy, and that direct communication between the people and their representatives could lead to the rule of demagogues and the mob. He agreed with James Madison that wise presidents should refine public opinion and promote thoughtful deliberation among the people and their representatives, rather than reflect the passions of the moment. Taft defended this view extensively in his collection of lectures, *Liberty Under Law: An Interpretation of the Principles of Our Constitutional Government* (1922). He emphasized that the Constitution included structural mechanisms, such as an independent judiciary, designed to slow the pace of direct democracy and to check "every temporary wind of popular passion."[16] As Taft emphasized,

> We are not a pure democracy governing by direct action, and the great men who framed our fundamental law did not intend that we should be. . . . The people do rule and always have ruled in the United States. They have their will but they have it after a wholesome delay and deliberation which they have wisely forced themselves to take under the restrictions of a Constitution which, adopted by however small popular vote, they have fully approved by more than one hundred and thirty years of acquiescence. It is this voluntary self-restraint that has made their Government permanent and strong. It is a fundamental error to seek quick action in making needed changes of policy or in redressing wrong.[17]

Taft inherited his devotion to constitutional fidelity over political expedience from his father, Alphonso Taft, who revered judges over politicians. After President Abraham Lincoln nominated Salmon Chase to be the sixth chief justice in 1864, Alphonso Taft told Chase, "To be Chief Justice of the United States is more than to be President, in my estimation."[18] Similarly, while signing Edward Douglass White's commission to become the ninth chief justice in 1910, President Taft lamented with characteristic honesty, "There is nothing I would have loved more than being Chief Justice of the United States. I cannot help seeing the irony in the fact that I, who desired that office so much, should now be signing the commission of another man."[19]

Both father and son served on the Ohio Superior Court and then achieved a series of increasingly high appointments at home and abroad. Alphonso Taft served as President Grant's secretary of war and President Benjamin Harrison's attorney general, as well as minister to the courts of Austria-Hungary and Russia. He was also a devoted party man who helped to found the modern Republican Party in 1856 on the principle of preserving the Union and the Constitution.

William Howard Taft passed on the same constitutional vision to his own children. Taft's oldest son, Robert Alphonso Taft, became one of the leading conservative senators of the twentieth century, celebrated as "Mr. Republican" for his advocacy of non-interventionism in foreign policy and his attempts to curb the power of labor unions. (The Taft-Hartley Act of 1947, which Robert Taft sponsored, outlawed the secondary boycott, or strikes by unions against companies that did business with other companies engaged in labor disputes, which William Howard Taft had fervently opposed as a lower court judge, as president, and as chief justice.) Robert Taft founded the modern limited-government wing of the Republican Party, in opposition to the big-government conservatism of President Dwight D. Eisenhower. William Howard Taft's daughter, Helen Taft Manning, distinguished herself as an American history professor, dean, and acting president at Bryn Mawr College. And his son Charles Phelps Taft II, known as "Mr. Cincinnati," served as Republican mayor of the Taft family's hometown.

If Americans today remember Taft for anything, it is likely for his weight: he is indelibly defined in the public mind as our largest president. The most famous photograph associated with Taft doesn't even include him: it's the one of four workers sitting in a giant bathtub that weighed a ton and was specially installed for Taft's use on the USS *North Carolina* during the president-elect's visit to the Panama Canal in January 1909. Taft had similarly large tubs installed on other battleships during his presidential excursions, although the claim that the president "would stick" in the bath and each time had to be "helped out," offered up by the White House usher Ike Hoover in his 1934 memoir,[20] has not been confirmed by any other contemporary source.[21] Still, cruel jokes about Taft and bathtubs abounded. The *Los Angeles Herald* ridiculed Taft by imagining that "some disrespectful, utterly mean person were to steal his clothes" while he was bathing and the president had to make his way home in an oversized barrel. The Chicago *Day Book* invited readers to give thanks Taft didn't take a bath with them.[22] The public's desire to observe Taft bathing became so irresistible that thrill-seeking citizens in Glenwood Springs, Colorado, in 1909 reportedly invited the president to wear a "specially constructed bathing suit" and to immerse himself in the public bath, an invitation Taft wisely declined.[23] Nevertheless, according to a report in the *New York Times* headlined "Taft Causes Hotel Deluge," Taft did, in fact, overflow a bathtub in Cape May, New Jersey, in 1915. "When he got into the tub the water overflowed and trickled down upon the heads of the guests in the dining room" below, according to the *Times*. "The entire resort, including Mr. Taft, laughed at the incident," and as Taft boarded the train the next morning, "he glanced at the ocean and said: 'I'll get a piece of that fenced in some day and then when I venture in there won't be any overflow.' "[24]

Taft's weight continues to be an object of public fascination: the Washington Nationals recently added Taft to the pantheon of "racing presidents" who scamper about to entertain the crowd, because he is credited with having started the tradition of the seventh-inning stretch as well as throwing out the first pitch in 1910. The Taft mascot was nicknamed "Big Chief," according to the *Washington Post*, and was made "a bit larger" than his polyurethane colleagues.[25] And yet, like many of his achievements, Taft's girth is taken out of context: for much of his life, Taft controlled his weight through impressive self-discipline. Taft was tall and large from youth—his nickname was not "Big Chief" but "Big Lub."[26] At his college graduation, he stood half an inch short of six feet and weighed 243 pounds, a weight that he carried gracefully.[27] (Taft was always an excellent dancer and sometimes waltzed alone on the White House veranda.) But he ate compulsively in times of stress, and by fall of 1905, when he was serving as secretary of war, he weighed 326 pounds.

Taft proceeded to lose 76 pounds in less than a year by rigorously following an Edwardian version of the Paleo diet, prescribed by the British physician Nathaniel Edward Yorke-Davies.[28] This remarkably effective diet forbade sugar, starch, dairy, and processed food while allowing unlimited quantities of green vegetables as well as small portions of lean meat or fish. By restricting himself to six hundred calories a day, Taft lost about 3 pounds a week between October 1905 and May 1906,[29] at which point he weighed 250 pounds.[30]

Having more or less starved himself for eight months, Taft ate his feelings in the stressful year that followed. He had abandoned his diet by 1907 and weighed 300 pounds during the presidential campaign of 1908. By the time he left the White House in 1913, he had ballooned to 340 pounds, his highest weight ever.[31] But after leaving the presidency, with contentment and relief, he resumed his Paleo diet and lost 75 pounds between March 1913 and March 1914. And he kept his weight down for the rest of his life, including his happy years as chief justice.[32] When he died in 1930 at the age of seventy-two, he weighed 244 pounds, only a pound more than he had weighed at his Yale graduation fifty years earlier.[33]

When Taft weighed over 300 pounds, in the Philippines and the White House, he likely suffered from obstructive sleep apnea, a disorder that jarred him awake every few minutes during slumber and made it impossible for him to enjoy a peaceful night's sleep. The result was somnolence throughout the day—he called it "that tendency to sleepiness which made me think of the fat boy in Pickwick"[34]—causing him to fall asleep on the campaign trail, during White House meetings with the chief justice and the wife of the French ambassador, at the opera, while playing cards, and even while standing at public events.[35] (Taft would snore loudly during these public naps, prompting Nellie and Archie Butt to awaken him with a kindly prod.) The disorder may have affected his ability to work for sustained periods during his presidency, leading to allegations of laziness among those who failed to appreciate its cause. Even Senator James Watson, who linked Taft's overeating and sleepiness in public with lack of executive focus, joked, after Taft jolted awake in his presence, "Mr. President, you are the largest audience I ever put entirely to sleep in all my political experience."[36] But after Taft's final Paleo diet at the end of his presidency, the sleep apnea disappeared, and he remained alert, focused, and remarkably productive for the rest of his happy career as a law professor and as chief justice.[37]

Taft was candid about his struggles with weight, and he responded to the relentless jokes with endearing good humor. He entertained crowds by telling stories on himself, including Secretary of War Elihu Root's famous telegram when Taft reported he was feeling fine in the Philippines after a long ride on horseback:

HOW IS THE HORSE?[38] Most striking of all, the president who viewed everything through a constitutional lens saw a connection between an unrestrained appetite for food and an unrestrained appetite for power. He gave a memorable speech as president comparing the struggle for self-control over one's diet to the struggle of popular majorities to exercise self-control in a democracy.[39] In the speech, titled "He Who Conquers Himself Is Greater Than He Who Taketh a City," Taft cited this proverb as an inspiration for men who struggled to control "the taste for strong drink" or "the appetite for food."[40] He went on to say that popular government, like personal fitness, is impossible unless the majority can muster self-control. In a true popular government, Taft declared, the people voluntarily embrace constitutional restraints on the expression of their will "to enable them to govern themselves, so that the first wave of popular will should not find immediate expression in legislation, but that the people should take time, should discuss the matter, and should have several delays before they accomplish their entire purpose with respect to the Government."[41]

"Taft will never be regarded as a great president, or even a good one," one commentator concludes, "but perhaps some day his obesity may cease to be his legacy."[42] In fact, Taft's ultimate success in mastering his own weight exemplified the self-discipline that he believed citizens in a constitutional republic had to find in themselves, in order to promote thoughtful deliberation rather than short-term gratification. This determination to use his leadership of the executive and judicial branches to promote thoughtful public deliberation and to protect the rule of law is, in fact, Taft's greatest legacy.

As I write, democracies around the world, including the United States, are engaged in a vigorous debate about whether populism—characterized by leaders who claim that they alone speak for the people—is consistent with constitutionalism—characterized by allegiance to representative government, checks and balances, individual rights, and the rule of law. New media technologies are enabling the rise of populist and nationalist political movements that threaten core constitutional values. Taft's legacy, therefore, is especially relevant today: as the only president to approach the office in constitutional terms above all, he provides a model for how presidents and justices can resist these pressures, which threaten judicial independence and the rule of law. Like the Framers of the Constitution, and like his heroes Hamilton and Marshall, Taft believed fervently that there is a tension between populism and constitutionalism. Like the Framers, he had studied failed democracies, such as Athens and Rome, and understood that direct democracy could lead to tyrants or demagogues who play on the passions of the mob.

Taft believed that democracy would perish if the people could express their preferences in initiatives and referenda, the precursors of today's Twitter polls or Brexit votes, rather than having their views filtered through constitutional structures and enlightened representatives, checked by independent judges to ensure thoughtful deliberation. And today, as populist politicians attack judicial independence, progressives are joining conservatives and libertarians in rediscovering the dangers of demagogic leaders who rule by executive order or pander to popular whims. In anxious times, Taft offers an unexpected and appealing model of a chief executive who took seriously the constitutional constraints on all three branches of government and, as chief justice, enforced those boundaries with vigor.

1

"A Judicial Temperament": The Education of Judge Taft

William Howard Taft inherited his judicial temperament and constitutional vision from his father, Alphonso Taft. A mutual acquaintance who heard the young Judge Taft hand down a decision exclaimed: "That young man has the judicial temperament, and the power of analysis and clear presentation of his father to an extent that is amazing."[1] Alphonso Taft was born on November 5, 1810, on a farm in Townshend, Vermont. He was graduated from Yale College and Yale Law School and then settled in Cincinnati, Ohio, where in 1841 he married Fanny Phelps, the cultivated daughter of a county judge. Two of their five children survived infancy: Peter Rawson Taft II and Charles Phelps Taft, who became a U.S. congressman and owner of the *Cincinnati Times-Star*, the Philadelphia Phillies, and the Chicago Cubs. Fanny died eleven years later, in 1852, and the following year Alphonso married Louisa Maria Torrey, a graduate of Mount Holyoke College, who later became a champion of women suffrage and free education.

As a delegate to the first Republican Convention, held in Philadelphia in 1856, Alphonso Taft voted for the first Republican platform, in which the delegates declared themselves opposed "to the extension of Slavery into Free Territory." Appalled that President Franklin Pierce had signed the Kansas-Nebraska Act of 1854, which allowed the extension of slavery into territories north of the line drawn by the Missouri Compromise, the delegates insisted that "the dearest Constitutional rights of the people of Kansas have been fraudulently and violently taken from them." And they resolved: "That the maintenance of the principles promulgated in the Declaration of Independence, and embodied in the Federal Constitution are essential to the preservation of our Republican institutions, and that the Federal Constitution, the rights of the States, and the union of the States, must and shall be preserved."[2] This resolution would define the political philosophy of both Alphonso and William Howard Taft, who was born the following year, on September 15, 1857, two days before the seventieth anniversary of the signing of the Constitution.

Alphonso and Louisa Taft's first son had died of whooping cough, steeling Louisa's determination for the survival of her second son, known as Will, who delighted his doting mother with his sunny temperament and good humor. "He is very large of his age and grows fat every day," his mother wrote of Taft as a baby. "He has such a large waist, that he cannot wear any of the dresses that are made with belts. He spreads his hands to anyone who will take him and his face is wreathed in smiles at the slightest provocation."[3] Three more children followed—Henry, Horace, and Fanny—and Will would consult them for political advice along his circuitous path to the White House and the Supreme Court.[4]

In 1851, Alphonso had bought a substantial Greek Revival house in Cincinnati with eight bedrooms and room for five Irish and German servants, where Will was born, grew up, and returned after college. The comfortable library in the Taft house still contains some of the law books that Alphonso and Will read together during Will's youth, filling the house with conversation about law and the Constitution. They include a first printing of the infamous *Dred Scott* decision published in 1857, the year of

Will's birth, with a handwritten notation on the cover calling attention to Justice Benjamin R. Curtis's dissent. Other books in the library include a *Political History of Slavery in the United States* and an early edition of the Lincoln-Douglas debates. Alphonso gave some of his law books to his protégé George Washington Williams, an African American politician, historian, and diplomat from Ohio, who later endorsed his nomination for governor in 1879 in these terms: "Judge Taft, the only white man in the Cabinet of any President during the last eighteen years who had the manhood, the temerity and humanity to exact . . . the powers of the Constitution of the United States to protect the black man in the exercise of his constitutional rights."[5]

On the Ohio Superior Court, Judge Alphonso Taft's most famous opinion was an 1870 dissent in a case about Bible reading in public schools. In the 1860s, the Cincinnati school board had banned the mandatory reading of the King James Bible in the classroom, after failing to resolve a conflict between Protestant and Catholic parents, who preferred the Douay version. A majority of the court struck down the ban, on the grounds that "revealed religion, as it is made known in the Holy Scriptures, is that alone that is recognized by our Constitution."[6] In his forceful dissent, Taft held that sectarian reading from the Protestant Bible was offensive to Catholics and Jews and represented an unconstitutional preference of one religion over another.[7] The Framers of the U.S. and Ohio Constitutions, he emphasized, intended to prevent the "union of Church and State." Following Alphonso Taft's reasoning, the Ohio Supreme Court unanimously reversed the Superior Court's decision in 1872, and nearly a century later the U.S. Supreme Court agreed that no sect may be preferred over another.[8] Alphonso may have been influenced by his Unitarian faith, which he passed on to his son. Will Taft later declared as much, with the admirable candor that often bedeviled his political career. "I am a Unitarian. I believe in God. *I do not believe in the Divinity of Christ*," he said, "and there are many others of the postulates of the orthodox creed to which I cannot subscribe."[9]

Alphonso lost the Republican nomination for governor to Rutherford B. Hayes in 1875 and lost again four years later; he blamed his defense of the separation of church and state for both defeats.[10] Both father and son viewed the political difficulties that resulted from unpopular constitutional rulings as a sign of their principled devotion to law rather than to politics.

His son was so sensitive to slights against his father's honor that when a newspaper editor published an item criticizing Alphonso Taft, Will confronted the editor on the street, lifted him up, and bashed his head repeatedly against the ground.[11] (These spasms of anger would recur throughout Taft's career, as he lashed out self-righteously against those he considered disloyal.) And Alphonso reciprocated his son's devotion. But Alphonso's dauntingly high expectations, combined with a habit of with-holding parental approval when his son failed to meet them, cre-ated a lifelong anxiety in Will that he expressed repeatedly in family letters. This pattern would continue when Will faced similarly conditional displays of approval from his demanding wife and from his political mentor Theodore Roosevelt. After Will ranked fifth in elementary school, for example, Alphonso declared: "Mediocrity will not do for Will."[12] Will did better at Woodward High School, graduating second in his class and earn-ing admission to Yale, his father's alma mater. While at Yale, Taft wrote anxiously to his father, "You expect great things of me, but you mustn't be disappointed if I don't come up to your expecta-tions."[13]

Taft's anxieties were increased by his tendency to procrasti-nate, requiring intense bursts of work as deadlines approached. But despite his inconsistent self-discipline—a tutor once wrote to his father that Will had received sixteen marks for irregulari-ties of attendance—he graduated second in his Yale class. (His half brother Peter had been first and their father, third.)[14] Like George Washington, Abraham Lincoln, and Theodore Roosevelt before him, Will Taft was an accomplished wrestler, winning the Yale heavyweight championship at his best college weight of 225 pounds.[15] He also joined Skull and Bones, the secret society his father had helped to found, and was considered the best debater at Yale. One of his teachers later recalled, "He was highly popular with the faculty because he used all his influence to dissuade his fellow students to keep out of scrapes. He always wielded his influence on the ground of order, decency, and common sense."[16]

In the fall of 1878, after graduating from Yale, Taft returned home to enroll in the Cincinnati Law School. While studying law, he worked as a court reporter for the *Cincinnati Commercial Tribune*, and his dispatches about the probate cases and domestic disputes in local courts were clear and well observed. During the summer of 1879, Taft worked in his father's law office, where Alphonso continued to chastise him for frivolous procrastinations, such as leaving the office early to watch the traveling Yale boat races. "I do not think you have accomplished this past year as much as you ought with your opportunities," his father wrote sternly. "Our anxiety for your success is very great and I know that there is but one way to attain it, & that is by self-denial and enthusiastic hard work in the profession."[17]

After graduating from law school in 1880, Taft became assistant prosecutor of Hamilton County, an appointment he owed to his father's political influence among Ohio Republicans. "What I really know of the law," Taft liked to declare, "I learned at the expense of Hamilton County, Ohio, as assistant prosecuting attorney, and judge of the Superior Court."[18] He had no interest in running for office but dutifully canvassed for Republican candidates.[19] As Taft's reputation for honesty and integrity grew, Congressman Benjamin Butterworth recommended to President

Chester Alan Arthur his appointment as collector of internal revenue for Cincinnati.[20] And so in January 1882, at the age of twenty-four, Taft left his job as assistant prosecutor to become the youngest tax collector in the country.[21] A contemporary profile described his appearance in admiring terms: "Personally, Mr. Taft is large, handsome and fair, with the build of a Hercules and the sunny disposition of an innocent child."[22]

As tax collector, the young innocent got his first taste of partisan politics, and it repelled him. When Governor Tom Young ordered Taft to fire several Revenue Department workers whom he thought were allied with his political opponent, Taft refused, protesting to the governor that the marked men were "among the best men in this District."[23] In March 1883, because of his abhorrence of corruption, he resigned his post as collector, although he continued to dabble in the politics of reform. Serving as chief supervisor of elections for Cincinnati, he was praised for his work in fighting voter fraud. Despite these accolades, Taft continued to recoil from politics, writing to his mother: "This is my last election experience I hope for some years to come."[24]

In 1884, enraged by a jury's refusal to hang a notorious murderer, a mob burned the Cincinnati Courthouse. The riot created in Taft a lifelong horror of mob violence and a determination to insulate the courts—and the presidency—from popular passions. And in his new position as assistant solicitor for Hamilton County, he accused a veteran trial lawyer, Thomas Campbell, of attempting to bribe one of the jurors. In his four-and-a-half-hour closing argument, Taft moralistically denounced Campbell for his lack of integrity and declared that the legal "profession must be kept pure."[25] Although Taft lost the case, he impressed Campbell's lawyer, Joseph Foraker, who would later be elected governor of Ohio and would support Taft's judicial ambitions.

As Taft's legal career thrived, he fell in love with a woman named Helen Herron, known as Nellie, who was four years younger and had contemplated forswearing marriage and becoming a teacher. Nellie's father, John Williamson Herron, had founded the Literary Club of Cincinnati in 1849, along with the future president Rutherford B. Hayes, his college classmate and law partner. (Alphonso Taft became an honorary member.)[26] John Herron served as a U.S. attorney and Ohio state senator but "twice declined appointments to the Bench," as Nellie recalled, "because the salary attached to these positions was not enough to support his large family."[27]

"The only incident of my girlhood which was in any way unusual," Nellie wrote in her memoir, *Recollections of Full Years*, "was my first visit to the White House as a guest of President and Mrs. Hayes."[28] It was, Nellie recalled, "a very important event. . . . I was not 'out,' so I couldn't spend my time in the White House as I would have liked, in going to brilliant parties and meeting all manner of charming people."[29] Still, the glamour of the experience made such an indelible impression, she told a journalist thirty years later, that she had returned from the White House and "confided to some of her girl friends that it was her purpose to marry only 'a man destined to be President of the United States.'"[30] And Nellie was not shy about sharing her purpose with others: when her family returned to the White House to celebrate the Hayeses' silver wedding anniversary in 1878, Nellie told "Uncle Rutherford" that she wanted "to marry a man who will be president." Hayes replied: "I hope you may, and be sure you marry an Ohio man."[31] That single-minded focus defined the seventeen-year-old Nellie's ambitions and would in time redirect those of her husband, whom she met the following year.

Will Taft and Nellie Herron were introduced at a coasting party, where he immediately took her down the hill on a bobsled. "I just heard Nellie say that you didn't sing so badly," his brother Horace teased soon after they met. "She must be in love with you."[32] Nellie especially remembered Will in a burlesque of *The Sleeping Beauty*, where he played the title role. In addition to amateur theatricals, Will relished discussing books with the intelligent and well-read Nellie; in an early letter, he advised her to reread the novels of Anthony Trollope "because of the realistic everyday tone which one finds in every line he writes."[33]

Their first lovers' quarrel, remarkably, was on a constitutional question—Nellie pressed her policy views on abolitionism, and Will opposed her on constitutional grounds—and his early missives read less like billets-doux than judicial opinions. "I am prepared to submit a few questions of this tenor to the high court of friendship wherein let Mr. Justice Taft and Miss Justice Herron to determine such questions,"[34] he wrote playfully. (Will was seeking Nellie's advice about whether it was ethical of him to have voted for a friend's father who sought a judgeship.) Still, his letters soon grew more ardent, and he proposed marriage at the end of April 1885. Nellie rejected him, following the custom of the day, but Will persevered, professing his love and unworthiness in a way that seems to reveal genuine insecurity rather than Victorian convention. When she demurred again two weeks later, he renewed his troth. "I know my faults, I know my weaknesses. I cannot justify or make light of what I confessed against myself," he wrote. "Oh how I will work and strive to be better and do better, how I will labor for our joint advancement if you will only let me."[35]

This last argument may have hit its mark. The next day, Nellie consented to an engagement "grudgingly rather than gratefully," in the words of her biographer, "as if she had granted a favor she was still reluctant to relinquish," and only on the condition that the engagement remain secret.[36] Will and Nellie were married the following year, on June 19, 1886. During their nearly forty-four years of marriage, he doted on his wife and repeatedly pleaded that he was unworthy of her love, while she reciprocated, like his father, by withholding the unconditional approval and affection that he craved. After receiving a letter from Nellie, Taft lamented that "there was no word of endearment or affection from one end to the other, and the tone of it sounded to me so hard and complaining."[37] But despite her high standards, Nellie always made her devotion to Taft clear. "I know that I am very cross to you, but I love you just the same," she once wrote him.[38] And Taft tenderly reciprocated Nellie's affection, kissing her in public with loud smacking noises that impressed his aide Archie Butt with their vigor.

Throughout their marriage, Nellie insisted that Taft pursue politics and forsake the bench. In March 1887, less than a year after their wedding, Taft excitedly told Nellie that Governor Foraker intended to appoint him to his father's old seat on the Ohio Superior Court. His wife did not share Taft's elation. "I dreaded to see him settled for good in the judiciary and missing all the youthful enthusiasms and exhilarating difficulties which a more general contact with the world would have given him," she wrote in her memoir, conceding that her husband "did not share this feeling in any way."[39] Taft accepted the appointment, and after a happy year of service, he was elected to a five-year term on the court, the only elected office he would hold until the presidency.

Taft took his seat on the Superior Court in 1887 at the age of twenty-nine, the youngest judge on the bench. Two years later, his first son, Robert Alphonso Taft, was born, and Taft handed down his most significant decision on the Superior Court, a case that would lead him to be denounced as "the Father of Injunctions" against organized labor. In *Moores & Co. v. Bricklayer's Union*, Taft held that union members seeking better working conditions may lawfully boycott their own employers but may not call for "secondary boycotts" against companies who do business with their employers. Applying this reasoning in the *Moores* case, Taft distinguished between legal and illegal boycotts by focusing on the question of malicious intent: the economic injury inflicted by the boycott, he wrote, "is a legal injury, or not, according to the intent with which it has been caused, and the presence or absence of malice in the person causing it."[40]

Reflecting his attempt to balance the interests of labor and capital, Taft would hold fast to this distinction between legal and illegal boycotts throughout his judicial and political career. In 1894, after he had been appointed as a federal circuit judge, Taft decided *Thomas v. Cincinnati, N.O. & T.P. Railway Co.*,[41] a case concerning the notorious Pullman railway strike. George Pullman, the American industrialist who developed the eponymous sleeper car,[42] had jacked up rents and slashed wages in his company town, causing his understandably aggrieved workers to strike.[43] In sympathy, Eugene V. Debs, president of the American Railway Union, responded by calling for a secondary boycott, announcing that his union would not operate any train in the country attached to a Pullman car. The railroad networks soon descended into chaos and bloodshed, as President Cleveland promised to call in federal troops.[44] (Debs would go on to run against Taft as the Socialist Party candidate for president in 1912; he was later imprisoned for his speeches denouncing World War I and ran again for president in 1920, this time from a jail cell.) Taft, who had a horror of mob rule, showed no sympathy for the strikers. In July 1894, he wrote to Nellie, "It will be necessary for the military to kill some of the mob before the trouble can be stayed."[45]

Later that month, the Cincinnati Southern railroad company sued for an injunction against Debs's colleague F. W. Phelan, accusing him of inciting workers to strike and preventing the railroad from pulling Pullman cars in defiance of its contractual obligations.[46] When Phelan defied the injunction, Taft issued a warrant for his arrest for contempt of court, and, in the *Thomas* case, he sentenced Phelan to six months in jail.[47]

In 1889, a vacancy had opened on the U.S. Supreme Court. With focused ambition, the thirty-one-year-old Taft asked Governor Foraker to recommend him for the seat, all the while acknowledging in a letter to his father that his odds were long: "My chances of going to the moon and of donning a silk gown at the hands of President Harrison are about equal."[48] Harrison decided not to nominate Taft to the Court, perhaps because of his youth and inexperience, but instead nominated him as solicitor general of the United States. Nellie was elated, convinced that accepting the job as the U.S. government's advocate before the U.S. Supreme Court would enable the couple to escape Cincinnati and to consort with a group she lionized as the Washington "bigwigs."[49]

Insecure about his speaking abilities, Taft castigated himself after his first oral argument before the Court. "I did not find myself as fluent on my feet as I had hoped to," he wrote to his father, adding that the justices "seem to think when I begin to talk that that is a good chance to read all the letters that have been waiting for some time [and] to eat lunch."[50] But hard work compensated for his lack of experience, and from 1890 to 1892 Taft won sixteen of his eighteen cases as solicitor general.[51] Taft also distinguished himself by introducing a noble practice in the solicitor general's office: "confessing error," or notifying the Supreme Court that, because of a constitutional or legal violation, the government should not have won its case. In 1891, at Taft's request, the Court reversed a murder conviction in Texas after Taft confessed that it had been based on hearsay evidence that should have been excluded.[52] The tradition of solicitors general "confessing error" continues to this day, and it is a tribute to Taft's honesty and his fervent belief that all conduct by the executive branch should conform to the Constitution and laws of the United States.

Alphonso Taft was proud, in the end, of his son's accomplishments. Taft wrote to Nellie that, on his deathbed, Alphonso "looked up at me in the sweetest way imaginable and said to me, 'Will, I love you beyond expression.'"[53] And Taft's career continued to thrive. By the end of his first year as solicitor general, Taft

had befriended Justice John Marshall Harlan, already distin-
guishing himself as the "great dissenter" from the Court's decisions denying civil rights.[54] He also developed close bonds with
President Harrison and Attorney General William Miller.[55] And
he struck up a close friendship with the new chairman of the U.S.
Civil Service Commission—that igneous force of nature Theodore Roosevelt.[56]

In March 1891, Congress created a new seat on the U.S. Court
of Appeals for the Sixth Circuit, in Ohio.[57] Taft's Republican
friends in Cincinnati organized a campaign on his behalf, and
Attorney General Miller and Justice Harlan called on President
Harrison to endorse him for the seat.[58] Nellie was dismayed by
the prospect of leaving Washington: "If you get your heart's
desire, my darling, it will put an end to all the opportunities you
now have of being thrown with the bigwigs."[59] But Taft preferred
the bench to the bigwigs, and in March 1892 he resigned as solicitor general to return to Cincinnati as a federal appellate judge.[60]
Taft would serve on the Sixth Circuit for eight happy years, while
also serving as a dean and professor of property at the Cincinnati Law School.[61] "I think he enjoyed the work of the following
eight years more than any he has ever undertaken," Nellie later
recalled, including the presidency.[62]

Although Taft professed to hate the publicity that resulted
from his closely watched opinion in the Pullman case, Nellie
relished her husband's labor opinions for raising his stock in
Republican circles.[63] And in February 1898, Taft decided another
landmark case, *United States v. Addyston Pipe & Steel Co.*, a decision reviving the Sherman Antitrust Act.[64] In 1890, with President Harrison's support, Congress had passed the Sherman Act
to prohibit anti-competitive behavior by monopolies. But corporations soon defied it, and the Supreme Court eviscerated it. In
United States v. E.C. Knight Co. (1895),[65] the Court held that
President Cleveland could not prosecute the Sugar Trust as a

monopoly under the Sherman Act because Congress had no power under the Interstate Commerce Clause of the Constitution to regulate the manufacture of goods, a purely intrastate activity, as opposed to their distribution across state lines.

In the wake of bipartisan support for trust busting, the government pursued the fight and prosecuted the steel pipe monopoly in the *Addyston* case. In 1894, the Addyston Pipe and Steel Company had agreed with five other iron pipe manufacturers to fix prices. The government charged illegal combination and conspiracy, but a lower court dismissed the case, noting that the Supreme Court had held that the Sherman Act did not apply to the manufacture of goods. When the case reached the Sixth Circuit, Taft held that the association among the six corporations was illegal because its main purpose was to restrain trade by creating a monopoly, and it did so not by regulating the manufacture of goods but by fixing prices for their sale.[66] Taft's decision made national news—the headline in the *New York Times* read, "Iron Pipe Trust Illegal: The First Case in Which Manufacturing Combinations Had Been Found Guilty."[67] The Supreme Court upheld Taft's decision in 1899,[68] affirming his emphasis on the illegal motive behind the combination, rather than examining the reasonableness of the fixed prices.[69] Relying on Taft's reasoning, Justice Rufus Peckham, a vigorous libertarian, held that the companies' liberty of contract had to yield to Congress's power to prohibit intentional conspiracies to create monopolies.

Taft distinguished between legal and illegal trusts in the same way he distinguished between legal and illegal union boycotts: by focusing on the question of malicious intent to interfere in what should be a free and fair market where labor and capital can compete on equal terms. The distinction reflected his moralism and distrust of labor unions as well as his moderation. Later, while campaigning for president in 1908, Taft explained in a speech that intentional monopolies could be banned because of the "badges of duress, badges of fraud" inherent in their character, but he clarified that "the mere aggregation of capital for economic purposes" was not illegal.[70] He celebrated *Addyston* as laying down "the principles upon which the Antitrust Law is now being enforced."[71] The case showed, he emphasized, "that the injunction works both ways"—against corporations and labor alike.[72]

___

2

"We Want Taft":
Civil Governor, Secretary of War,
and President-Elect

In January 1900, as Judge Taft was enjoying the comforts of the federal bench, he received an unexpected telegram from President William McKinley summoning him to Washington.[1] There was no open seat on the Supreme Court, and so Taft wondered what the president wanted to discuss. At the White House, McKinley greeted Taft warmly. He told the judge that he had created a commission to oversee civil government in the Philippines, which the United States had annexed at the end of the Spanish-American War. He wanted Taft to join the commission and perhaps even to lead it.[2]

Taft was astounded. Years later, he would say that McKinley might as well have told him "that he wanted me to take a flying machine."[3] (Taft often expressed his surprise at presidential appointments by imagining that he had been ordered to take flight.) Taft protested to McKinley that he spoke no Spanish and had questioned the wisdom of annexing the islands.[4]

"Why, I am not the man you want," Taft declared. "To begin with, I have never approved of keeping the Philippines."

"You don't want them any less than I do," McKinley replied, "but we have got them and in dealing with them I think I can trust the man who didn't want them better than I can the man who did."[5]

Taft could never ignore a call to duty. But one question mattered to him above all others: Would this mean the end of his judicial career? On this point, the president was reassuring. "All I can say to you is that if you give up this judicial office at my request you shall not suffer," McKinley said. "If I last and the opportunity comes, I shall appoint you" to the Supreme Court.[6] The judge who revered Alexander Hamilton and John Marshall was especially excited by the prospect of framing and interpreting a new constitution for the Philippines.[7]

Still, after leaving the meeting, Taft agonized as usual about his preference for the security of the bench over the indignities of political combat. "I confess that I love my present position," he wrote to his brothers. "Perhaps it is the comfort and dignity and power without worry I like."[8] The question summed up what would become his personal dilemma over the next eight years: he yearned to be chief justice, but his wife and his brothers were determined to make him president. Taft resolved that he could not give up life tenure on the bench without being given authority as well as responsibility, and so he accepted the assignment on the condition that he lead the commission.[9] Nellie later acknowledged that her husband's resignation from the circuit court was "the hardest thing he ever did."[10]

On April 17, 1900, the Tafts and their three children set out from San Francisco for the Philippines on the USS *Hancock* with the four other members of the Philippines commission: a former Confederate general, a New England judge, a University of Michigan zoologist, and a University of California historian.[11] This colorful delegation stopped off in Tokyo, where the commissioners were received by the Japanese emperor and empress. On June 3, the American commissioners arrived at Manila Bay to a frosty reception from General Arthur MacArthur. Recently appointed as military governor of the islands, the general insulted the commissioners by refusing to greet them in person.[12] MacArthur commanded the sixty-five thousand American troops who were attempting to quell the Philippine guerrilla insurrection that had begun in 1899, and he resented the intrusion on his powers. Taft framed the dispute in constitutional terms, defending the president's authority to delegate power to civil or military authorities as he saw fit.[13] The commission opened for business in September 1900, with Taft as its president. Five months later, Congress declared the insurrection over and transferred power from military to civilian authorities.[14] On June 21, 1901, McKinley appointed Taft civil governor of the Philippine Islands. (He was also known as the governor-general.) The Taft family moved into the stately Malacañan Palace, and Nellie was "well pleased with the idea of living in a palace," as she confessed in her memoir, "however unlike the popular conception of a palace it might be."[15]

For Taft, the chance to live in a palace was less enticing than the chance to act as a solon, a constitution maker bringing the blessings of liberty to a grateful people. In the spirit of American federalism, Taft decentralized power and added Filipino representatives to the Philippine Commission. And he scrupulously implemented the Philippine Organic Act of 1902, the law passed by Congress to govern the islands, which extended to the Filipino people a list of the rights guaranteed in Article I of the Constitution, including the right of habeas corpus, which allows prisoners to challenge the legality of their detentions. The act also extended to the Philippines most of the guarantees of the U.S. Bill of Rights, with two significant exceptions: the right to bear arms and the right to trial by jury.[16] In testimony to Congress, Taft explained why he agreed that it would be "a great mistake" to extend to the Filipino people these basic means of defending their own liberties. The right to jury trial and the right to bear arms, he declared, "should be withheld from the people until they learn a self-restraint that can only be learned after practice, and the advantage of the example of self-government which, by a gradual course, we hope to give them."[17]

Taft's testimony summed up his fervent if paternalistic view that only those who took the time to acquire self-discipline through education were capable of self-government. He concluded, therefore, that the Constitution did not always follow the flag into conquered territories such as Puerto Rico and the Philippines. The Supreme Court had recently decided the same question in the *Insular Cases* (1901), which held that the Dingley Tariff, a landmark American statute imposing tariffs on a series of manufactured goods, did not extend to the Philippines. Taft applauded the decision, both because he felt that the tariff would hurt the island's economy and because he felt that the Filipino people should be granted the full rights of the Constitution only when they were ready to exercise them responsibly.

Broadly, the debate in the United States over whether the Constitution followed the flag reflected a larger moral debate. Jeffersonian anti-imperialists, such as the Democratic presidential candidate William Jennings Bryan and the Republican senator George F. Hoar of Massachusetts, insisted that imperialism abroad, like slavery at home, denied the conquered people the natural, God-given rights of equality and liberty promised by the Constitution and the Declaration of Independence.[18] Hamiltonian imperialists, such as the progressive Republican senator Albert Beveridge of Indiana, insisted that Americans were divinely entitled to govern the Philippines without the people's consent.[19]

Taft, as usual, stood between the two constitutional extremes. He told Theodore Roosevelt, "I did not agree with Senator Hoar and his followers, that the Philippines were capable of self-government or that we were violating any principles of our government or the Declaration of Independence so far as they were concerned, that I thought we were doing them great good."[20] At the same time, he disagreed with Beveridge that America had a duty to civilize what the senator considered an inferior race without their consent. Instead, Taft maintained that the Filipinos should be granted as much involvement in all three branches of government as their level of education allowed. As he declared in his inaugural address as civil governor, delivered on July 4, 1901, his ultimate goal was to make the "islands ripe for permanent civil government on a more or less popular basis."[21]

Taft patronizingly referred to Filipino people as "our little brown brothers" and believed that the majority of them were "utterly incapable of self-government and should the guiding hand of the United States be withdrawn, chaos, conscription and corruption would follow inevitably," a view he attributed to the chief justice of the Philippine Supreme Court.[22] But he was less condescending than the imperialists and the U.S. military, which marched defiantly to the words: "He may be a brother of William H. Taft but he ain't no friend of mine!"[23] Recognizing that the Filipinos were sensitive to slights, or any implication of inferiority,[24] Taft insisted on treating them as social equals. The Tafts hosted a public "at home" reception every Wednesday in the governor's palace and advertised it in the leading newspapers. By asking the Filipinos "personally and persistently to 'be sure and come Wednesday,'" Nellie recalled, "we prevailed on a good number to believe they were really wanted; and after a little while there began to be as many brown faces as white among our guests."[25]

Taft's democratic initiative was so successful that he became surprisingly popular among the Filipino people. In fact, on many levels, Taft was a striking success as civil governor. He thrived in an atmosphere where he could serve as both chief executive and chief judge, enforcing congressional statutes like a benign magistrate. He encouraged the commission to hold open hearings on new legislation, which he helped to draft.[26] Without a legislature to check him, or political rivals to criticize him, Taft could have taken liberties in shaping the Philippines as he saw fit.[27] But Taft applied his old habits of judicial deference in fulfilling his executive duties, and he worked to implement the goals of Congress and the president, rather than imposing his own.[28]

Under Taft's leadership, the commission revised the old Spanish tax code, built new roads and harbors, established a health department, police force, and independent judicial system—the judges were divided between Americans and Filipinos, as Taft put it, to "enable the Filipinos to learn and administer justice."[29] Most significantly, reflecting his views about the importance of education in making self-government possible, Taft built a series of public schools that, within years, taught more native Filipinos to speak English than Spanish. Nellie wrote that Taft's establishment of first-rate public schools received more "enthusiastic support and co-operation" from the Filipino people than any other of her husband's projects.[30] "Whatever may be said about the American Constitution," she declared happily, "there can be no dispute about the fact that education follows the flag."[31]

Back in the United States, Theodore Roosevelt was feeling emasculated as William McKinley's vice president. "I had a great deal rather be your assistant in the Philippines . . . than be vice-president," he wrote to Taft in August 1900.[32] After hearing of Taft's promotion to civil governor, he wrote a prophetic profile of Taft in *Outlook* magazine, noting that "the first Governor of the Philippines ought to combine the qualities which would make a first-class President of the United States with the qualities which would make a first-class Chief Justice of the United States." Roosevelt concluded, "The only man . . . who possessed all these qualities was Judge William H. Taft, of Ohio."[33] Taft reciprocated Roosevelt's praise, writing to the vice president, "I have no doubt that you will be the [presidential] nominee in 1904."[34] Roosevelt did not wait long. On September 14, 1901, William McKinley died eight days after he had been shot by an assassin at the Pan-American Exposition in Buffalo. Roosevelt learned at dawn that he was now president of the United States.

On October 26, 1901, after scarcely a month in office, Roosevelt urged his friend to accept a Supreme Court appointment. WOULD APPRECIATE EARLY REPLY, he cabled impatiently to Taft in Manila.[35] But as much as he craved the position, Taft felt a duty to the Filipino people at a time of economic crisis, and this compelled him to resist temptation. GREAT HONOR DEEPLY APPRECIATED BUT MUST DECLINE, Taft responded.[36] Roosevelt tried to accept Taft's demurral with grace, replying, "If possible, your refusal on the ground you give makes me admire you and believe in you more than ever."[37] In private, however, Roosevelt bristled at Taft's inflexible sense of duty: "I have never in my life felt like criticizing anything that Will did, but, upon my word, I do feel like criticizing this mental attitude of his!"[38]

At the end of 1901, Taft endured two dangerous operations to remove an abscess on his intestines. While in Washington for a third surgery, he met with Roosevelt, who said he hoped Taft would complete his work in the Philippines before the next Supreme Court vacancy came up. In January 1902, Taft had recovered sufficiently to testify before a Senate committee for two hours, answering hostile questions about alleged cruelty used by American military forces while quelling the rebellion led by the Filipino nationalist Emilio Aguinaldo.[39] Taft always became defensive in the face of criticism, but here he was self-aware enough to acknowledge his vulnerability. "It shows my unfitness for public life for me to dislike [the attacks] so and be so sensitive about them," he observed to Nellie. "I suppose it indicates a thin-skinned vanity."[40]

The following month, President Roosevelt dispatched Taft to Rome, where the civil governor conducted delicate and successful negotiations with Pope Leo XIII over the sale of four hundred thousand acres in the Philippines held by Spanish friars.[41] (The vast scope of the land seized by the Church had provoked a Philippine revolt against Spanish rule before the Americans arrived.) Nearly two years later, the United States would agree to pay $7.5 million for most of the lands instead of taking them by force, another diplomatic triumph for Taft.[42] During the trip, Taft's family joined him for an audience at the Vatican. When the pope asked young Robert Taft about his intentions, the boy channeled his father, replying that he meant to become chief justice of the United States.[43]

In January 1903, Roosevelt tried once again to appoint Taft to the Supreme Court. And Taft replied once again that he recognized "a soldier's duty to obey orders," but pleaded that he be allowed to complete his unfinished business in the Philippines.[44] In the meantime, Filipino leaders, and the people themselves, demonstrated outside the Malacañan Palace for Taft to stay. "The whole city of Manila was placarded, in all the necessary languages, with the simple and uniform sentiment: 'Queremos Taft,' 'WE WANT TAFT,'" Nellie recalled, adding that Secretary of War Elihu Root's "rendering of this in English was 'I want you, Mah Honey, yes, I do.'"[45] In the face of this gratifying demonstration, Taft agreed to stay put; never again would he experience such fervent popular affection. On January 13, Roosevelt conceded petulantly, "All right, you shall stay where you are."[46]

Two months later, Roosevelt asked Taft to replace Root as secretary of war, stressing that he could continue to administer the islands from Washington.[47] "If only there were three of you!" Roosevelt added flatteringly. "Then I would have put one of you on the Supreme Court . . . one of you in Root's place as secretary of war, when he goes out; and one of you permanently governor of the Philippines."[48] This time, Taft's family convinced him to accept the post. His generous half brother Charles, who had married the heiress to an iron fortune and supported Taft throughout his political career, even offered to supplement Taft's cabinet salary to help defray the costs of living and entertaining in Washington. And Nellie, whose eye was always on the White House, was happy to return to Washington as the wife of a cabinet officer.[49] And so on December 23, 1903, Taft set off for Washington from Manila on the SS *Korea*.

Roosevelt still wanted to put Taft on the Court, now viewing the appointment as part of his effort to ramp up federal antitrust enforcement. His most dramatic crusade was against the Northern Securities holding company, a giant conglomerate merging the shipping and rail lines of Morgan and Vanderbilt with those of Rockefeller, Harriman, and Gould. After the merger, Northern Securities became the world's second-largest corporation, surpassed only by U.S. Steel, which J. P. Morgan also controlled.[50] "If we have done anything wrong," Morgan protested to the president, "send your man to my man and they can fix it up."[51] Roosevelt retorted that he wanted to stop the Northern Securities merger, not fix it, prompting Morgan to ask whether U.S. Steel was vulnerable to a lawsuit as well. Roosevelt replied that the Steel Trust was safe "unless we find out that in any case they have done something that we regard as wrong."[52] And the president kept his word. During the Panic of 1907, a leading brokerage house that owned a large stake in the Tennessee Coal, Iron, and Railroad Company threatened to go bankrupt. In exchange for Roosevelt's assurances that the government would not file an antitrust suit against U.S. Steel, Morgan offered to restore financial stability by buying the Tennessee combination, in what turned out to be a sweetheart deal.

Taft enthusiastically supported Roosevelt's decision to prosecute the shipping and railway trust in the *Northern Securities* case, and he sat in the Supreme Court with Attorney General Philander Knox on March 14, 1904, as Justice Harlan announced the Court's 5–4 decision holding that the trust had illegally restrained commerce in violation of the Sherman Antitrust Act.[53] Taft must have been proud as Harlan cited the Supreme Court decision upholding his own reasoning in the *Addyston* case. Justice Oliver Wendell Holmes Jr., whom Roosevelt had appointed in 1902 when Taft turned down the seat, voted against the administration in the *Northern Securities* case, prompting the president to exclaim, "I could carve out of a banana a judge with more backbone than that."[54]

As head of the War Department, Taft was now in charge of overseeing the Philippines, pacifying Cuba, and supervising the construction of the Panama Canal. Roosevelt declared himself happy to leave Washington for a hunting trip in the Rockies because he had "left Taft sitting on the lid."[55] In 1904, Taft set off for Panama to oversee progress on the canal and impressed all with his vitality, attention to detail, and keen administrative ability.[56] He also stumped for Roosevelt in the 1904 presidential campaign and was relieved when Roosevelt won—although he confessed prophetically that "a national campaign for the presidency is to me a nightmare."[57]

During Roosevelt's second term, Taft traveled to Havana to quell an insurgency, briefly becoming provisional governor in 1906.[58] A magazine profile called him "the proconsul of American good faith to fractious islands; an ambassador to stubborn tasks at far corners of the earth."[59] In addition to proving his gifts as an able administrator and chief operating officer, Taft was also a natural consensus seeker.[60]

When he wasn't traveling, Taft brightened the offices of the War Department in Washington with his laughter and good humor.[61] The work must have been more congenial than his executive duties in the Philippines; starting in October 1905, Taft found the iron self-discipline to lose seventy-six pounds.[62] Here is a typical day on the Taft diet, in the words of his diet guru, Dr. Yorke-Davies. At 8 a.m., "you may sip a tumbler of hot water," adding "a squeeze of lemon if liked." At 9 a.m., Taft breakfasted on "two or three of gluten biscuits"—in other words, gluten-free biscuits—and six ounces of "lean grilled steak or chop, or of chicken, or of grilled kidney, or of grilled or broiled white fish." Lunch at 1:30 allowed "4 or 5 ozs of lean meat," such as beef, mutton, lamb, "or of chicken or game in season, or of rabbit or turkey"; and "4 or 5 ozs of carefully cooked green vegetable, without butter"; and "3 or 4 ozs of baked apple or stewed apple or other fresh fruits." Salad could be "taken freely, but no oil is allowed," along with one of the gluten-free biscuits. In the afternoon, a cup or two of coffee or tea could be taken, "if liked," but without milk or sugar, "or a cup of beef tea." Finally, for dinner at 7, Taft could enjoy "clear soup when desired," meat, fish, and vegetables, and stewed fruit in the same quantities as at lunch and "salads as in the list if liked (no oil) and two of the biscuits."[63] The low-carb diet hit its mark, and within seven months Taft had returned to his college weight. "A reduction of seventy pounds is not an inexpensive luxury,"[64] Taft wrote to Nellie, lamenting the $400 he owed his tailor.

Still, even during his happy tenure at the War Department, Taft pined to be chief justice. In 1906, when the retirement of Justice Henry Billings Brown opened yet another Supreme Court vacancy, Taft wrote in his diary, "I am very anxious to go on the Supreme bench. The President has promised me a number of times that he would appoint me Chief Justice if a vacancy occurred in that position and he knows that I much prefer a judicial future to a political future."[65] Nellie, however, viewed Roosevelt's 1906 offer of an associate justiceship as an attempt to take Taft out of the running for president, and she insisted that he reject it. A friend of the family asked Taft's son Charlie whether his father would accept the Supreme Court seat. "Nope," he replied, because "Ma wants him to be president."[66]

Later that year, Taft and Nellie joined the Roosevelts for an intimate dinner at the White House, after which Roosevelt threw himself into a chair in the library and closed his eyes.

"I am the seventh son of a seventh daughter and I have clairvoyant powers," he intoned melodramatically. "There is something hanging over his head. I cannot make out what it is. . . . At one time it looks like the Presidency, then again it looks like the chief justiceship."

"Make it the presidency," said Mrs. Taft.

"Make it the chief justiceship," said Mr. Taft.[67]

In December 1907, Roosevelt issued a statement reaffirming his promise not to seek a second full term, a pledge he had rashly made on the night of his election in 1904 and soon came to regret. Taft quietly stumped for the Republican nomination by courting the state delegations, and in time he bested his main rival, Governor Charles Evans Hughes of New York. Taft's only misstep during the quiet campaign was his impulsively candid response in January to a reporter's question about what he would do for those unemployed in the wake of the Panic of 1907. "God knows," Taft replied. "They have my deepest sympathy. It is an awful case when a man is willing to work and is put in this position."[68] (The phrase "God knows" was quoted out of context, provoking public outrage.) Thanks to Roosevelt's steadfast support, in June 1908 the Republican Convention in Chicago nominated William Howard Taft to be its candidate for president of the United States. The Texas delegation brandished a flagpole with a pair of plus-sized trousers, accompanied by the slogan "As pants the hart for cooling streams, so Texas pants for Taft!"[69] A series of five photographs taken of Taft on the telephone at the moment he received word of his nomination from President Roosevelt shows his face, serious at first, crinkling into a contented grin.

Roosevelt, who had learned of Taft's nomination during a tennis game, quickly issued an enthusiastic endorsement: "I do not believe there can be found in the whole country a man so well fitted to be president."[70] Months later, in an interview with *Success Magazine* entitled "Why the President Is for Taft," Roosevelt was even more effusive. "The bigness of the job demands a man of Taft's type," he explained. "Never has there been a candidate for president so admirably trained in varied administrative service." All this was entirely accurate. But Roosevelt added two predictions that proved to be overly optimistic. "I think Taft will succeed better with Congress than I have done," and "I sincerely believe that Taft will make our greatest president, excepting, of course, our two greatest, Washington and Lincoln."[71]

In 1908, Roosevelt and Taft were the closest of allies, and Taft promised to put Roosevelt's sweeping executive actions on firmer legal footing. Far from viewing himself as Roosevelt's clone, Taft said that his constitutional vision would make his agenda "distinct from, and a progressive development of," his predecessor's agenda. "The chief function of the next Administration," he declared, in his speech accepting the Republican nomination on July 28, "is to complete and perfect the machinery by which these standards may be maintained, by which the lawbreakers may be promptly restrained and punished, but which shall operate with sufficient accuracy and dispatch to interfere with legitimate business as little as possible."[72]

After a two-hour parade in his honor, Taft addressed the enthusiastic crowd from a special reviewing stand constructed in front of his brother Charles's grand colonial home in Cincinnati. Taft's acceptance speech lasted an hour but hit its mark. (The *Wall Street Journal* praised it as "an exceedingly able and shrewd political document" that positioned Taft "in the middle of the road, avoiding alike the extreme of eastern conservatism and the extreme of western radicalism.")[73] Verbose and legalistic, like all of his prose, his acceptance speech is not light reading— Taft wrote as he thought—but he was remarkably transparent as he judiciously weighed all sides of each argument and candidly shared the strengths and weaknesses of his conclusions. In the end, Taft's speeches, like judicial opinions, reward the patient reader. They amount to detailed constitutional contracts with America about the legal reforms Taft intended to bring about.

The Democrats were led for the third time by the populist barnstormer William Jennings Bryan. The "Great Commoner" had championed free silver in 1896 and anti-imperialism in 1900 and was determined to make the 1908 campaign a referendum on Republican domestic financial reforms.[74] America had just recovered from the Panic of 1907, when the stock market dropped by more than 50 percent, only to be rescued by J. P. Morgan, who pledged his own capital to shore up confidence. The Democratic platform of 1908 declared that the panic showed that the Republicans were "either unwilling or incompetent to protect the interests of the general public."[75]

Taft promised to continue Roosevelt's reform policies, and he and Bryan agreed on the need to curb the power of the trusts. But they disagreed about how to go about curbing that power. In his acceptance speech, Taft rejected the Democrats' efforts to prevent monopolies from forming in the first place by imposing caps on size, banning trusts that controlled more than 50 percent of a product's market, and requiring national licensing for trusts that controlled more than 25 percent. Instead, Taft returned to the definition of illegal trusts he had championed as a judge: to be unlawful, he said, a trust has to display "an element of duress in the conduct of its business," based on the illegitimate "purpose of controlling the market, to maintain or raise prices, restrict output and drive out competitors."[76] Taft proposed vigorous antitrust prosecutions, including injunctions against illegal trusts and criminal prosecutions against the corporate officers, to bring the trusts "within the law."

On the central economic issue in the campaign, the Democrats supported tariffs only for the purpose of raising revenue, not for the protection of American industries. Taft embraced the promise in the Republican Party platform to preserve the protective tariff but also to reduce it. He pledged to call a special session of Congress immediately after the inauguration to revise the tariff in accordance with "the true principle of protection"— namely, "the imposition of such duties as will equal the difference between the cost of production at home and abroad, together with a reasonable profit to American industries."[77]

On the rights of labor, the Democratic platform vigorously

opposed judicial injunctions against striking unions, and Bryan campaigned as the champion of labor.[78] Taft, on the other hand, had been denounced as the "Father of Injunctions," and he maintained his support for property rights throughout the campaign. Taft adhered to the position he had taken as a judge: that "workmen have a right to strike" and to persuade their co-workers to join them, "provided it does not reach the point of duress." But they may not "injure their employer's business by use of threats or methods of physical duress" or by "a secondary boycott against his customers or those with whom he deals in business."[79]

On the need to publicize corporate campaign contributions, Taft largely agreed with the Democrats, noting that the Republican Congress in 1907 had banned "contributions from corporations to influence or pay the expenses connected with the election of presidential electors or of members of Congress." He personally refused to accept questionable campaign contributions from large corporations, prompting Roosevelt, who had been less fastidious, to write, "My affection and respect for you are increased by your attitude about contributions. But really I think you are oversensitive." Taft also pledged to support a federal law requiring the disclosure of "contributions received by committees and candidates in elections for members of Congress, and in such other elections as are constitutionally within the control of Congress." But he did not endorse the Democratic call for "the enactment of a law prohibiting any corporation from contributing to a campaign fund and any individual from contributing an amount above a reasonable maximum."[80]

Finally, Taft tepidly endorsed the proposal in the Democratic platform for a constitutional amendment that would authorize the direct election of senators; although he said a federal income tax amendment was not strictly necessary, he would later endorse it as well. (Congress would propose both amendments during his presidential term.)

At the end of his exhaustive acceptance speech, Taft apologized for its length with endearing modesty.[81] Nellie, who often upbraided him for writing speeches that read like judicial opinions,[82] was excited afterward. "Hasn't it been glorious! I love public life," she exclaimed. "To me this is better than when Mr. Taft was at the bar and at the bench, for the things before him now and in which he takes part are live subjects."[83] Still, Nellie was correct that Taft's 1908 campaign speeches read like judicial opinions.[84] How was it possible, with such dry and legalistic speeches, that Taft could win a comfortable popular victory—51 percent to Bryan's 43 percent—over the most celebrated orator of his day?

One clue comes from the excerpts of his acceptance speech that Taft recorded for the Edison Record Company on August 3, 1908, just a few days after his notification ceremony. The election of 1908 was the first time that sound recordings played a central role in a presidential campaign, and they were distributed in an unusual way. Taft and Bryan supporters often held "record duels," inviting other supporters to listen to the recordings of both candidates in a church hall or public meeting place. A newspaper in Spokane, Washington, described one of these battles of the phonograph: a Bryan supporter played Bryan's recording on the need to reduce the tariff, only to be interrupted by a Taft supporter playing the song "Merry Ha Ha." The Taft man would then play Taft's warning that "taking the tariff off on all articles coming into competition with the so-called trusts would not only destroy the trusts, but all of their small competitors," and the Bryan man responded with a recording of the comic song "Oh Glory," in which the Bryan supporters lustily joined.[85]

The new technology was undeniably exciting, converting even the most tiresome speech into an exhilarating novelty. But in addition to their unexpected entertainment value, the Bryan and Taft records make clear that Taft's legalistic delivery was well matched to Bryan's more orotund style, and uniquely well suited to the acoustical recording methods of his day. Bryan's delivery has a grandiloquent and stentorian quality—he trills his *r*'s on words like "Orient" and "experiment"—but the Great Commoner's recordings sound more natural than his flamboyant rerecordings of his 1896 "Cross of Gold" speech.[86]

In his final speech, titled "Mr. Taft's Borrowed Plumes," Bryan accused the accommodating Taft of adopting some of his best ideas from the Democratic platform.

He favors an income tax when we need it, but thinks we do not need it now. . . . Mr. Taft favors railroad regulation. . . . Mr. Taft is personally inclined towards the election of senators by the people. . . . Mr. Taft advocates a certain kind of publicity, of campaign contributions. . . . Mr. Taft is advocating tariff revision. . . . Mr. Taft even recognizes that the Filipinos must ultimately have independence.

Bryan's conclusion: "Mr. Taft has [even] imitated the Democrats in using the talking machine as a means of reaching the public."

Bryan was correct: Taft's speeches for Edison, recorded three months later, stole some of Bryan's dramatic and substantive thunder. In the twelve recordings, Taft's baritone is calm, unaffected, and entirely American—he has no regional inflection, except for his pronunciation of the word "man-a-facture." His diction, like his prose, is modest and judicious, and always respects the intelligence of the listener. And in his speeches responding to Bryan, Taft did indeed embrace some aspects of the Democratic platform, including one that Roosevelt had ignored: a call to preserve the Constitution. In the election of 1904, Taft noted, the Democrats had focused on "the usurpation of the powers of the Executive Office for President Roosevelt including his settlement of the anthracite coal strike and the violation of the federal constitutional limitations by the Republican Party." The people, however, rejected the Democratic "party which had temporarily assumed its ancient character as a preserver of the

Constitution."[87] Quoting from his acceptance speech, Taft promised again to put Roosevelt's executive orders on firm legislative and constitutional grounds. Taft also promised to reorganize the Department of Justice and the Department of Commerce and Labor, noting that "the moral standards set by President Roosevelt will not continue to be observed by those whom cupidity and the desire for financial power may tempt, unless the requisite machinery is introduced into the law."[88]

In the rest of his recorded speeches, Taft's focus was more legal than political. Unlike the openly segregationist Democrats, he unequivocally endorsed the Republican platform's "demands [for] justice for all men without regard to race or color" and "for the enforcement and without reservation in letter and spirit of the Thirteenth, Fourteenth, and Fifteenth Amendments to the Constitution." He called for the restraint (but not the destruction) of unlawful trusts. Invoking the reasoning of his own lower court opinions, he endorsed the right of unions to strike but denounced the secondary boycott.

In one recording, Taft's personality unexpectedly shines through. The topic, of all things, was Irish humor. After quoting Kipling about how, in Ireland and America, "smiles and tears chase each other fast," Taft offered a surprisingly personal recollection of a trip to County Cork twenty-five years earlier. "We landed at Queen Sound very early in the morning of a July day and it seemed to me that nothing was ever greener, nothing was ever sweeter, nothing was ever more attractive than the surroundings of Queen Sound harbor at that hour." Taft then recited "the musical verse *The Shandon Bells*," which crowded his memories at the time:

> With deep affection and recollection
> I oft times think of those Shandon Bells
> Whose sounds so wild would, in days of childhood
> Fling round my cradle their magic spells.

In reciting these verses, Taft's voice is somber yet rhapsodic. He recites beautifully and deliberately, in tones he must have used when reading aloud to Nellie during their courtship. The spirit revealed by this intimate act of personal revelation is vulnerable and sentimental, earnest and full of soul.

On November 3, 1908, Taft was elected the twenty-seventh president of the United States. He carried twenty-nine of the forty-six states, won 321 electoral votes to Bryan's 162, and out-polled Bryan by more than a million popular votes.[89] On the night of his victory, Taft gave a short speech. "I pledge myself to use all the energy and ability in me to make the next Administration a worthy successor to that of Theodore Roosevelt. I could have no higher aim than that," he said.[90] In fact, he did have a higher aim—to preserve, protect, and defend the Constitution of the United States.

3

"The Best Tariff Bill":
The President, Tax Reform,
and Free Trade

On March 3, 1909, the day before Taft's inauguration, President Roosevelt invited his successor to spend the evening at the White House. Waiting for Taft's arrival as the sun set over Lafayette Park, Roosevelt confided his doubts to the journalist Mark Sullivan. "He's all right," the president replied when asked how Taft would make out. "He means well and he'll do his best. But he's weak."[1] At dinner, Nellie expressed elation and the Roosevelt party gloom. Taft then ducked out to attend a Yale smoker at the Willard Hotel, before returning to the White House after midnight to find Nellie awake with excitement. Preparing for bed in the Blue Room, which had previously served as President Lincoln's cabinet room, she found a plaque declaring, "In this room Abraham Lincoln signed the Emancipation Proclamation of January 1, 1863, whereby four million slaves were given their freedom and slavery forever prohibited in these United States."[2] "It seemed strange," she recalled, "to spend my first night in the White House surrounded by such ghosts."[3]

Early the next morning, Taft and Roosevelt met for breakfast before venturing into icy streets, covered by the heaviest snow in twenty years. "Well, Will, the storm will soon be over,"

Roosevelt exclaimed. "As soon as I am out where I can do no further harm to the Constitution it will cease." "You're wrong," Taft replied. "It is my storm. I always said it would be a cold day when I got to be President of the United States."[4] Both predictions—about the constitutional threats that Roosevelt had posed in his effort to impose his program by executive fiat and the personal and political toll of Taft's efforts to repair them—would prove to be correct.

Because of the blizzard, the ceremony outside the Capitol was canceled for the first time since the inauguration of Andrew Jackson. Taft took the oath in the Senate Chamber instead.[5] He made a point of swearing on the same Bible that Supreme Court justices had used for decades.[6] (When Taft returned the Bible to the Court, he vowed that he would use it again if he ever took the oath as a justice himself.)[7] After repeating the presidential oath along with Chief Justice Melville Fuller, who flubbed the wording, William Howard Taft became what he, like the Framers of the Constitution, called the chief magistrate of the United States.

Taft released his inaugural address to the press but mercifully did not read it in its entirety. (The spoken excerpts were sufficiently brief that his son Charles didn't feel the need to open the copy of *Treasure Island* that he had brought for diversion in case his father's address bored him.)[8] In his written draft, Taft made clear that he viewed the promises in what he called his "letter of acceptance" of the Republican nomination, like those in the Republican platform, as enforceable contracts with the public that he meant to perform. "A matter of most pressing importance is the revision of the tariff," he declared. "In accordance with the promises of the platform upon which I was elected, I shall call Congress into extra session to meet on the 15th day of March, in order that consideration may be at once given to a bill revising the Dingley Act,"[9] the last major tariff bill, passed by Congress in 1897, which had raised tariffs by an average of 57 percent. "The Republican party declares unequivocally for a revision of the tariff by a special session of Congress immediately following the inauguration of the next President,"[10] the 1908 Republican platform had declared. On the campaign trail, Taft emphasized that he would strictly construe the word "immediately."[11]

Taft suggested that Congress focus solely on tariff reform at the extra session, "to secure the needed speed in the passage of the tariff bill." But believing, as he did, that the president had the constitutional authority to recommend legislation to Congress but no authority to interfere with Congress's power to legislate, Taft emphasized, "I venture this as a suggestion only, for the course to be taken by Congress, upon the call of the Executive, is wholly within its discretion."[12] The tariff bill, Taft stressed above all, should try to achieve a balanced budget rather than protectionism for its own sake.[13] The federal government had an obligation to be "as economical as possible" in its spending, and "to make the burden of taxation as light as possible."[14]

Taft, in other words, was more of what would later be called a deficit hawk than Roosevelt, who during his last full year in office had increased government expenditures by $80 million, resulting in a deficit of $57 million.[15] In 1909, the deficit had risen above $89 million, and Taft insisted on fiscal discipline. In his first annual message to Congress he would declare, "Perhaps the most important question presented to the Administration is that of economy in expenditures and sufficiency of revenue."[16] As a result of Taft's directive to cut costs, the various cabinet departments slashed nearly $50 million in spending in 1909.[17] The cost cutting, combined with increased revenue from a corporation tax that Congress passed the same year at Taft's recommendation, had its effect. The federal deficit shrank to $11 million in 1910, and Taft achieved surpluses of $11 million in 1911 and $3 million in 1912.

Taft ended his inaugural address on a characteristically judicial note, pledging to uphold "the power of the federal courts to

issue injunctions in industrial disputes." Here, Taft was implicitly rebuking his predecessor on a topic that foreshadowed their
coming breach. In his final message to Congress, Roosevelt had
criticized judges who "often fail to understand and apply the
needed remedies for the new wrongs produced by the new and
highly complex social and industrial civilization which has grown
up in the last half-century."[18] This assault on the courts struck
at the heart of Taft's most fervent beliefs.

As soon as Taft finished speaking, Roosevelt rushed up to
shake his hand, exclaiming something that sounded to Mrs. Taft
like "Bully speech, old man!"[19] The former president then hur-
ried out of the room. Soon after the inauguration, as Roosevelt
set off for an African safari, Taft wrote him a thoughtful note
accompanied by an inscribed golden ruler. "I want you to know
that I would do nothing in the Executive Office without considering what you would do under the same circumstances and
without having in a sense a mental talk with you over the pros
and cons of the situation," he wrote to "My dear Theodore,"
whom he was still inclined to call "My dear Mr. President."[20]
With keen self-awareness, Taft acknowledged that he was not as
adept as Roosevelt in working with journalists to explain his policies and educate the public. "I fear that a large part of the public will feel as if I had fallen away from your ideals; but you know
me better and will understand that I am still working away on
the same old plan."[21] Roosevelt jotted off a quick reply as the SS
Hamburg left New York: "Am deeply touched by your gift and
even more by your letter. Greatly appreciate it. Everything will
turn out all right, old man. Give my love to Mrs. Taft."[22]

When she walked into the White House for the first time as
first lady, Nellie felt "as Cinderella must have felt when her mice
footmen bowed her into her coach and four and behaved just as
if they had conducted her to a Court Ball every night of her life."
She experienced "a little secret elation," which quickened as she
stood over the brass seal with the national coat of arms sunk into

the floor of the entrance hall: "'The Seal of the President of the United States,' I read around the border, and now—that meant my husband!"[23]

The Tafts enjoyed an inaugural lunch, followed by a tea for the president's Yale classmates, the inaugural parade, and a ball at the Pension Building. They returned to the White House at one o'clock in the morning, and Nellie's last memory before she fell asleep was a hearty laugh from her husband as she asked drowsily, "I wonder where we had all better have breakfast in the morning!"[24] Reviews of Taft's inaugural address were positive. The *New York Times*, which had pledged to support the Union, the Constitution, and Reconstruction after the Civil War but had moved away from the Republican Party during the scandals of the Grant administration, accurately predicted, "We are to have, it seems, during the next four years, a government of laws, of laws enforced by an Executive of a just and deliberating mind."[25]

Taft initially felt like something of an imposter in the White House. "When I hear someone say Mr. President," he declared on March 11, "I look around expecting to see Roosevelt."[26] And yet Taft wasted no time doing precisely what he had promised during his campaign: he set out to put Roosevelt's policies on sound legal ground that respected the constitutional boundaries established by the Framers. As he had explained in January, "We do not wish to destroy that government or so change it as to make it different from that which our fathers and forefathers contemplated in the formation and maintenance of the Constitution, entered upon in 1789."[27] But because he approached many decisions as a principled judge rather than a calculating politician, he immediately stepped into political minefields. The trouble began with the selection of his cabinet. As Taft recalled, "One day, just after I was nominated, I told Roosevelt, that should I be elected, I did not see how I could do anything else but retain all the old members of the Cabinet."[28] But, a few months later, Taft changed his mind and decided to replace the old Roosevelt loyalists with a cabinet of what he called "corporation lawyers" who could help him in his constitutional tasks.

As Taft told his new secretary of state, Philander Knox, who was one of the corporation lawyers, "I am trying . . . to act as judicially as possible, and to free myself from considerations of friendly association as far as I can and remain a decent man with red blood in me."[29] Rather bloodlessly, however, Taft sacked Roosevelt's secretary of the interior, James R. Garfield, son of the late president and one of Roosevelt's staunchest supporters, because he questioned the legality of some of Garfield's decisions—made in concert with Gifford Pinchot, the head of the U.S. Forest Service—to withdraw land for federal conservation.[30] Taft's decision to replace Garfield with Richard Ballinger, the Seattle reform mayor turned corporate lawyer, would lead Pinchot to retaliate, precipitating the biggest scandal of his presidency.

All told, Taft nominated six corporate lawyers to his cabinet: Knox as secretary of state, Ballinger as secretary of the interior, George Wickersham as attorney general, Jacob Dickinson as secretary of war, Frank Harris Hitchcock as postmaster general, and Charles Nagel as secretary of commerce and labor.[31] Only the two holdovers from Roosevelt's cabinet—Secretary of Agriculture James Wilson and Secretary of the Navy George von Lengerke Meyer—along with Taft's new secretary of the treasury, Franklin MacVeagh, had escaped legal training.[32] "I am going to be criticized for putting corporation lawyers into my Cabinet," Taft accurately predicted, as critics such as Henry Adams wondered why a president elected to carry out Roosevelt's policies had fired most of Roosevelt's men.[33]

Taft soon settled into a calmer, more judicious work schedule than his frenetic predecessor, whom Adams had described as "pure act." The president's days started at 7:00 a.m., when he ate what his aide Archie Butt recalled as "a hearty breakfast" that often included a twelve-ounce steak.[34] (The gluten-free biscuits had disappeared.) By 9:30, he left for the new White House Oval

Office, which Taft himself had designed and installed in the West
Wing in October 1909 to replace the temporary executive office
that Roosevelt had constructed. A rudimentary air-conditioning
system, using three thousand pounds of ice a day to pipe cold air
into the Oval Office, ensured the smiling president's comfort, even
on the warmest summer days.[35] He often skipped lunch, except
for an occasional apple, Butt recalled, but "I don't think this
fast does him any good, for he eats a correspondingly larger dinner. He has a tremendous appetite and does not control it as
did his predecessor."[36] Exhausted by sleep apnea and fleeing the
pressures of office, he liked to escape in the afternoon for golfing,
horseback riding, or, with increasing pleasure, motoring. Continuing his schoolboy habits of procrastination, Taft worked in
concentrated bursts, waiting until the last minute and then producing a prodigious volume of speeches and reports. But Taft's
work habits as president were also shaped by his work habits as
a federal judge. He presided over cabinet meetings as if they were
judicial conferences. He weighed all sides of an issue before reaching his verdict without consulting others. He based his decisions
on legal rather than political considerations. And he handed down
his decisions in speeches and messages to Congress that read like
judicial opinions, without considering their political effect.[37]

True to his promise to Roosevelt and the American people,
Taft set out immediately to revise the tariff. On March 16, 1909,
as he had pledged in his inaugural address, Taft invoked his
constitutional authority to summon both Houses "on extraordinary Occasions" and convened a special session of Congress. The
Senate and House waited expectantly as the clerk began to read
Taft's presidential message. But when the clerk finished reading
after two minutes, the assembled members of Congress were
astounded. They had anticipated a state paper of historic importance and presidential leadership, but Taft had sent them a 340-
word message that he had composed in fifteen minutes that
morning.[38]

The message urged Congress "to give immediate consideration to the revision of the Dingley Tariff Act." Taft explained that the current tariff was insufficient to raise enough revenue to pay government expenditures; without adjustment, there would be a deficit of $100 million by the next July. Moreover, because the Republican Party had pledged to revise the tariff, and the business community and the country expected the pledge to be fulfilled, those expectations had created "an extraordinary occasion, within the meaning of the Constitution, justifying and requiring the calling of an extra session."[39] Taft reminded Congress that his inaugural address had outlined the principles of tariff revision and new taxation to avoid future deficits. "It is not necessary for me to repeat what I then said," he concluded. "The less time given to other subjects of legislation in this session, the better for the country."[40]

Read in light of Taft's constitutional understanding of the limits of his own powers, his brief message is a masterpiece of concision. Taft believed that the Constitution gave him the power to recommend to Congress "consideration of . . . such measures as he shall judge necessary and expedient."[41] And that is precisely what he had done in his inaugural address, which many of the statesmen had heard and all could read. He believed that Congress alone could decide whether to accept or reject his suggestions. What more needed to be said?

In fact, Taft had stepped into a political minefield so explosive that even the ordinarily bellicose Roosevelt had been too fainthearted to approach it. Roosevelt believed, with the progressives, that high tariffs led to higher prices and more entrenched monopolies, but he feared igniting a tariff battle that would divide eastern manufacturers in protected industries, who favored the tariff, from western farmers, who paid higher prices for raw materials, such as oil and steel, and therefore opposed it.[42]

Moreover, the question of what kind of taxes should fund the national debt was one of the central constitutional debates of the

American republic. Since the Founding era, most federal revenue had come from import taxes raised by the tariff and excise
taxes on staples such as sugar and salt; by 1910, these taxes funded
90 percent of the federal budget. That's because the Constitution required that all "direct taxes" be apportioned according to
population rather than according to personal wealth or property.
When the tariff failed to raise enough revenue, excise taxes on
goods such as whiskey and carriages filled the gap. Although they
were often unpopular with the consumers (and had provoked the
1791 Whiskey Rebellion), the Supreme Court had upheld the
constitutionality of excise taxes in the 1796 *Hylton* decision,
argued by Alexander Hamilton.[43]

One way to avoid contentious debates over tariffs, which had
divided the North and South in the years leading up to the Civil
War, was to adopt a temporary income tax. In 1861, after
the South seceded from the Union, the Lincoln administration
imposed the first federal income tax, a flat tax of 3 percent on
all incomes over $300 a year, to fund the Civil War.[44] Neither
Abraham Lincoln nor his secretary of the treasury, Salmon
Chase, whom Lincoln would later appoint chief justice, believed
that an income tax was a "direct tax" that had to be apportioned
among the states according to population.[45] And after the war
the unpopular income tax expired.

The idea of an income tax had support, however, among
Democrats as well as Republicans. After the Panic of 1893, populist Democrats argued that tariffs and excise taxes were regres-
sive instruments of economic tyranny that discriminated against
farmers and the producing classes. The Democratic Congress,
supported by a Democratic president, Grover Cleveland, passed
a federal income tax bill in 1894 that included a 2 percent tax
on incomes over $4,000, as well as tariff reductions. But the
Supreme Court wasted no time in striking down the law by a
5–4 vote in the *Pollock* case (1895),[46] on the ground that taxes

on income were direct taxes that had to be apportioned among the states. In doing so, the Court disregarded the reasoning of the 1796 *Hylton* decision, which held that only taxes that could plausibly be apportioned according to population—such as taxes on land or head taxes—qualified as direct taxes. Taft, then a federal circuit court judge, agreed with Justice Harlan's dissent in *Pollock*, which exhaustively reviewed the records of the Constitutional Convention to argue convincingly that the Framers intended direct taxes to encompass only taxes on land and slaves.

The *Pollock* case was the most controversial of its day. It made the federal income tax impossible to administer, since the people of Delaware, if they represented 4 percent of the U.S. population, would have had to pay 4 percent of the income tax.[47] It also cleared the way for Congress to raise the tariff to fund the national debt. Goaded by the popularity of President William McKinley's protectionist policies, Congress passed the Dingley Tariff of 1897, setting rates as high as 50 percent. (European rates were closer to 10 percent.) During the 1908 presidential campaign, Taft acknowledged, "One of the great policies to which the Republican Party has been pledged from the beginning has been the protective system."[48]

Nevertheless, at the beginning of Taft's presidency, this consensus among Republicans had begun to splinter. Recent articles by the muckraking journalist Ida Tarbell helped to galvanize a bipartisan political revolt against protectionism, as consumers came to recognize that they were paying higher prices for domestic as well as imported goods, because domestic manufacturers could jack up prices without fear of foreign competition. By March 1909, when Taft sent his terse message to Congress, he faced a three-way struggle among competing camps of tariff reformers within the Republican Party. Moderate Revisionists, like Taft himself, wanted to reduce but not eliminate tariffs, returning to the original Hamiltonian vision of modest import duties as sources of revenue.[49] Insurgent Republicans, led by progressives such as Senator Robert La Follette of Wisconsin, wanted to reduce tariffs even further, to increase competition and lower consumer prices, although they did not go so far as free trade Democrats to argue that the tariff should be eliminated entirely. And standpat Republican protectionists, led by Speaker Joe Cannon, who controlled the majority of Republican votes in the House, and the powerful senator Nelson Aldrich of Rhode Island, wanted to maintain or even increase the rates of the Dingley Tariff. "Where did we ever make the statement that we would revise the tariff downward?" Aldrich asked Taft disingenuously, ignoring the fact that everyone understood the promise of tariff revision in the Republican platform as a pledge to reduce the rates, not simply to change them in one direction or the other.[50]

These warring Republican factions might have defeated even the shrewdest and most determined politician. But Taft in this case was no politician at all, insisting that the Constitution prohibited him from interfering with Congress's deliberations. "I have no disposition to exert any other influence than that which it is my function under the Constitution to exercise," he told Aldrich, unwittingly tipping his hand.[51] He could have supported the effort by the insurgent Republicans to unseat Speaker Cannon, but he viewed the encouragement of an intraparty coup as beyond his constitutional authority as well. "I would be very severely criticized," he protested, "if I should attempt to use executive power to control the election in the House."[52] In this way, Taft used his devotion to the Constitution, and to party unity above all, to justify his temperamental aversion to building congressional support for his legislative agenda. After submitting his brief to Congress, he was content to wait for Congress's verdict.

He did not wait long. Sereno E. Payne, the chairman of the House Ways and Means Committee, was, like Taft, a Republican moderate who supported downward revision based on the difference between the costs of production at home and abroad.[53] On the day Taft sent his brief message to Congress, Payne introduced a tariff revision bill, reflecting more than a year of hearings. In a nod to Taft, he proposed to eliminate duties on coal, hide, and iron ore, while more than doubling duties on gloves—an industry of Payne's home state of New York.[54] Taft praised the Payne bill, calling it "as near [to] complying with our promises as we can hope," and the bill passed the House on April 9.[55] In the Senate, however, the bill was eviscerated by nearly eight hundred amendments sponsored by Senator Aldrich, more than half of which restored rates to the levels of the Dingley law.[56]

Even if Taft had been inclined to intervene in this battle, which he was not, he was soon distracted at home. Nellie Taft had settled into her role as first lady with enthusiasm and style. She replaced the white ushers in frock coats at the front door of the White House with African American ushers in blue livery. She installed oriental furnishings (including the constitutionally controversial tapestry from Japan) and tropical plants throughout the executive mansion, prompting servants to refer to it as the Malacañan Palace.[57] And she left a permanent and welcome mark on Washington, D.C., by accepting the gift of three thousand Japanese cherry trees from the mayor of Tokyo and planting them around the Tidal Basin in 1910. When the trees bloomed the following year, and she saw the cherry blossoms, Archie Butt reported, "Mrs. Taft actually clapped her hands in delight."[58]

Soon after moving into the White House and achieving her most ardent dream, however, Nellie Taft collapsed during an outing on the presidential yacht.[59] "I was permitted fully to enjoy only about the first two and a half months of my sojourn in the White House," she wrote decorously in her memoir. "In May I suffered a serious attack of illness and was practically out of society through an entire season."[60] In fact, Nellie had suffered a terrible stroke, which deprived her of control of her right arm and leg, and her power of speech. Seeing his paralyzed wife carried into the salon, Taft "went deathly pale," as Archie Butt recalled, adding that "the President looked like a great stricken animal. I have never seen greater suffering or pain shown on a man's face."[61] During the year that it took Nellie to recover her ability to speak, Taft nursed her with patience and loving attention, working with her gently for hours a day. A housekeeper recalled that he was always full of laughter in an effort to ease her strain. "Now please, darling, try and say 'the'—that's it, 'the,'" he would say. "That's pretty good, but now try it again."[62] Nellie thrived under Taft's tender ministrations, and after a substantial recuperation, she looked "lovely and happy," as Archie Butt observed her during one of Taft's speeches. "She always looks happy when listening to the President."[63]

The Tafts had a summer home in Beverly, Massachusetts, which was known during Taft's presidency as the "Summer Capital of the U.S." As Nellie recuperated there, the president was left alone in the White House to observe the fight over the tariff bill from a distance. He drew one line in the sand: unless Congress revised the tariff downward, he would veto the bill.[64] Always most comfortable as a conciliator presiding over a judicial conference, he then invited the House and Senate conference committees to the White House for dinner on the veranda—the press called it the "White House lovefeast"—where he scrupulously avoided discussing substantive issues, which he considered Congress's prerogative.[65]

In the end, the wily Aldrich assured Taft that his views would be duly considered, and although Taft confessed he could not predict the outcome—"I am trusting a great many of them," he told Nellie, "and I may be deceived"—he decided his duty to the Constitution and to the unity of the Republican Party required him to defer to Aldrich, who did indeed deceive him. When the conservative protectionists finally passed a bill that increased hundreds of duties while decreasing others, La Follette, the leader of the insurgents, rushed to the White House and urged the president to assert himself. "Well, I don't much believe in a president's interfering with the legislative department while doing its work," Taft replied with judicial blandness. "They have their responsibility and I have mine."[66] On July 15, he rejected demands that he throw down the gauntlet and threaten a veto, declaring, "I could make a lot of cheap capital by adopting just such a course, but what I am anxious to do is to get the best bill possible with the least amount of friction. I owe something to the party, and while I would popularize myself with the masses with a declaration of hostilities toward Congress, I would greatly injure the party and possibly divide it."[67]

On August 5, 1909, convinced that the Payne-Aldrich bill was consistent with the promise in the Republican platform to revise the tariff, Taft signed it into law. Although disappointed that the bill didn't go further, Taft viewed it with equanimity. "I hope that my attitude will have so reconciled the people of this country as to make them believe, what is a fact, that the bill really is a good bill," Taft wrote to Nellie. "It does not go far enough in certain respects, but it goes far in others; and a tariff bill no one can be entirely satisfied with."[68] With judicial precision, he gave several speeches emphasizing that, all things considered, the bill represented a downward revision: there were 654 decreases, 220 increases, and 1,150 unchanged items, and the average duty on imports was 21.09 percent, whereas under the Dingley law it had been 24.03 percent.[69]

Taft argued plausibly that the bill—the first downward revision of the tariff since the Cleveland administration—was the best he could have achieved, given the explosiveness of the politics.[70] The *Washington Post* agreed. "It is easy to pick flaws in the bill, but it cannot be denied that, as a whole, it is as good as any tariff legislation that has preceded it," the editors declared.[71] But the progressive press attacked the bill as a capitulation to big business, reinforcing the public perception that Taft had sided with the conservatives over the insurgents.[72] And it's true that Taft was sometimes willing to veto bills that offended that Republican orthodoxy—such as the populist Democratic free trade bill—but he refused to veto the Payne bill after it was diluted by Aldrich's amendments. In the end, Taft was more devoted to preserving the unity of the Republican Party than to offering presidential leadership. But instead of uniting the party, his insistence that the Constitution precluded him from interfering with the details of legislation ultimately divided it.

Nevertheless, Taft achieved the tariff revision that eluded Roosevelt, and he shaped the tax reforms of the Payne-Aldrich bill as well. In a fiscally responsible search for additional federal revenue to balance the loss of funding from the tariff, the House proposed a graduated federal inheritance tax, which Taft had endorsed in his inaugural address. The Senate objected on the ground that some states viewed a federal inheritance tax as a form of double taxation, since they already imposed state inheritance taxes of their own.[73] Taft then called on Congress to adopt an ingenious compromise: a 2 percent tax on corporate net profits and the constitutional amendment authorizing an individual income tax that would not require apportionment. He had criticized the Supreme Court's *Pollock* decision in 1895 as depriving the federal government "of a power which, by reason of previous decisions of the court, it was generally supposed that Government had."[74] But he also believed that passing another income tax statute would embarrass the Court, since the justices were unlikely to reverse themselves, and his devotion to the Court's legitimacy trumped his own constitutional views. In the meantime, Taft viewed the 2 percent excise tax on corporate income as a temporary solution that would allow Congress to raise revenue and regulate corporations at the same time.[75]

As Taft told Congress, "It is the constitutional duty of the President from time to time to recommend to the consideration of Congress such measures as he shall judge necessary and expedient."[76] And on this front, Taft's recommendations were largely successful. In July 1909, Congress passed a resolution calling for an amendment to the Constitution authorizing Congress to collect income taxes. And in 1911 the Supreme Court would unanimously uphold the corporate tax as an indirect tax on the privilege of doing business as a corporation, rather than a direct tax on income.[77] All in all, despite criticism from extreme reformers, Taft had cause for wan satisfaction with the Payne-Aldrich bill. He had set the United States down a path of tax reform that, in time, would lead to a bipartisan consensus favoring relatively free trade and a federal government funded by an income tax rather than by protective tariffs.

In the late twentieth century, the journalist Michael Kinsley observed that a gaffe in Washington involves a politician inadvertently telling the truth. The compulsively honest Taft wrote many of his own speeches without editing, and he often embarrassed himself when his truth-telling gaffes were taken out of context. In a Memorial Day appreciation of Ulysses S. Grant delivered during the 1908 campaign, Taft scandalized an audience of veterans by declaring that, before the Civil War, Grant had "resigned from the Army because he had . . . yielded to the weakness of a taste for strong drink."[78] (A few sentences later, Taft added that Grant eventually had "overcome in a great measure his weakness for strong drink,"[79] but the qualification was lost in the uproar.) And shortly after he signed the tariff bill, Taft committed what proved to be the most politically damaging gaffe of his career.

In September 1909, Taft decided to tour the country for a few months, to "get out and see the people and jolly them."[80] Taft's attempts to jolly the people consisted of delivering nearly forty speeches—all of them read like long, technical judicial opinions—on topics ranging from corporation taxes to the environment. "I do not think his speeches will read as well when put in book form as they will be pleasing to those communities in which they

were delivered," Butt accurately predicted as the tour began, noting that Taft began the trip as a labored and anxious speaker
but increasingly gained confidence.[81] One of his first stops was
in Winona, Minnesota, the home of James A. Tawney, the chairman of the House Appropriations Committee, who wanted the
president to offer an unequivocal endorsement of the Payne-
Aldrich tariff bill.[82] On Constitution Day, September 17, Taft
responded like a lawyer arguing a case. He later explained that
he had written his speech on the tariff hastily the night before,
but his last-minute effort produced the equivalent of a legal brief,
with exhaustive charts and numbers comparing the new tariff
with the old and establishing that the new bill reduced more
tariffs than it raised.

"I did not promise that everything should go downward," Taft
declared accurately. "What I promised was, that there should be
many decreases, and that in some few things increases would be
found to be necessary; but that on the whole I conceived that
the change of conditions would make the revision necessarily
downward—and that, I contend, under the showing which I have
made, has been the result of the Payne bill."[83] He acknowledged
that the bill was not perfect. But the words that followed would
come back to haunt him for the rest of his career.

> On the whole, however, I am bound to say that I think the
> Payne tariff bill is the best tariff bill that the Republican
> party ever passed; that in it the party has conceded the
> necessity for following the changed conditions and reducing
> tariff rates accordingly. This is a substantial achievement
> in the direction of lower tariffs and downward revision,
> and it ought to be accepted as such.[84]

These two sentences are a classic Kinsley gaffe. As Gilbert and
Sullivan's Yeomen of the Guard exclaimed in a hearty chorus

on another topic, "Every word of them is true." Moreover, Taft went on to emphasize that, although he thought the bill was not perfect, he had signed it in the interest of party unity, which he thought was the precondition for "representative government" in America. But given progressive demands for more dramatic tariff reform, even Taft's tepid defense of the bill struck them as political heresy, for it suggested that no better bill was possible. As usual, however, Taft did not consider the political implications of his candor. "He no longer apologizes. He accepts, he defends, he is enthusiastic," the *New York Times* fulminated.[85] Wrenched out of context, Taft's praise of "the best tariff bill that the Republican Party ever passed" went viral on the wires.

The press accounts failed to note that Taft's defense of the bill was also based on his commitment to government by party. Taft understood, as the historian Sean Wilentz has noted, that the great movements for social change in America have come from strong political parties that unite groups with different interests.[86] Taft insisted that "in a party those who join it, if they would make it effective, must surrender their personal predilections on matters comparatively of less importance." As a loyal Republican, he said, he could do no less.[87]

On the remainder of the tour, Taft defended the rest of his balanced tax policy. In a speech on corporation and income taxes, delivered in Denver on September 21, he said the only way to balance the budget was to cut expenditures or increase revenues, and he pledged his administration would do both, beginning with cutting expenditures by up to $50 million.[88] Taft noted, however, that with the tariff reductions in the new law, some tax increases were necessary to make up the deficit. Although Taft believed that "the Constitution does not forbid the levying of an income tax by the Central Government," he had supported the compromise reached by Senate Republicans, passing the corporation tax and proposing the constitutional amendment authorizing a federal income tax. Because he feared that citizens who disagreed with a federal income tax might refuse to pay and then commit perjury to avoid prosecution, Taft believed that an income tax should be imposed only in times of emergency, as in the Civil War.[89] And he disagreed with liberals and populists who wanted to use the income tax "for the purpose of permanently restraining great wealth."[90]

After leaving Colorado (where he declined to wear the specially constructed bathing costume at Glenwood Springs),[91] Taft continued to Utah and then to the West Coast, with stops in Seattle, San Francisco, and Los Angeles. He then set off for Texas and Mexico, where he toasted the capitalist dictator Porfirio Díaz.[92] This was the first visit to Mexico by an American president and Taft's first excursion into "dollar diplomacy," or a foreign policy designed to advance America's business interests. "I am glad to aid him," he wrote to Nellie, "for the reason that we have two billions [of] American capital in Mexico that will be greatly endangered if Díaz were to die and his government go to pieces."[93] As it happened, the government did go to pieces: the idealistic revolutionary Francisco I. Madero would overthrow President Díaz just eighteen months later. Still, Taft's visit produced at least one decent joke. When his aides expressed relief that Taft had escaped Mexico without an attempted assassination, the president replied with a ready smile, "If anyone wanted to get me, he couldn't very well have missed such an easy target."[94]

In Taft's final speeches of his tour, he reflected on the limits of his constitutional powers as president. In an address, "Wisdom and Necessity of Following the Law," delivered at the state fairgrounds of Macon, Georgia, on November 4, Taft embraced a strikingly restrained conception of the presidency. "The thing which impresses me most is not the power I have to exercise under the Constitution, but the limitations and restrictions to which I am subject under that instrument."[95] He also denounced presidential efforts to circumvent Congress's will through executive orders: "The best way of getting rid of a legal limitation that interferes with progress . . . is to change the law, and not rely upon the Executive himself to ignore the statutes and follow a law unto himself."[96]

4

"Within the Law":
The Environment, Monopolies,
and Foreign Affairs

President Taft was determined to put President Roosevelt's policies on protecting the environment, prosecuting the trusts, and keeping the peace on firm legal and constitutional grounds. When his efforts ignited a political firestorm, the judicial president was unprepared to extinguish it.

A disagreement about how to protect the environment provoked the first conflagration. Roosevelt had issued executive orders to protect from development millions of acres of national forest. But in 1908, Congress, influenced by corporate interests, tried to thwart Roosevelt's conservation efforts by passing a law transferring the power to establish national forests from the president to Congress.[1] Roosevelt was undaunted by constitutional formalities. In the waning days of his presidency, working with his secretary of the interior, James R. Garfield, and his chief forester, Gifford Pinchot, he issued a midnight executive order protecting from hydroelectric power development more than a million additional acres of land.[2] Roosevelt justified the withdrawal under his "stewardship" theory of executive power, insisting that the president could do anything the Constitution didn't explicitly forbid.[3]

Garfield and Pinchot offered no resistance to the president's wishes, determined as they were to restrict, by any means necessary, the access of giant corporations to forest lands and water reserves. Pinchot, the first head of the U.S. Forest Service, was a moralistic crusader—initially for the conservation of land and later for the prohibition of alcohol.[4] He viewed Roosevelt's efforts to regulate the water power trust as only one battle in the holy war between the people and the monopolies. A future secretary of the interior, Harold Ickes, would dub him "Sir Galahad of the Woodlands."[5] Even after the repeal of Prohibition, as governor of Pennsylvania, Pinchot ended his career moralistically denouncing the evils of alcohol. In an irony that seemed to escape him, however, he designed a state-run monopoly on the sale of liquor that continues to frustrate lovers of intoxicating spirits in the Keystone State to this day.

Taft, too, was committed to conservation, but he was also committed to the rule of law. As he wrote to Pinchot, "I am thoroughly in sympathy with these policies and propose to do everything that I can to maintain them, insisting only that the action for which I become responsible . . . shall be within the law."[6] Taft promptly asked Congress for federal legislation codifying Roosevelt's executive orders.[7] Congress responded enthusiastically to Taft's expression of respect for its constitutional prerogatives and restored executive power over land conservation. In the end, Taft would withdraw more land for federal protection in his single term in office than Roosevelt did in two terms, protecting 8.5 million acres and creating ten national parks.[8] As the historian Jonathan Lurie notes, Taft called himself a "progressive conservative"[9] and meant to preserve rather than threaten Roosevelt's legacy. But Taft's achievements would be overshadowed by a dramatic clash between Pinchot and Taft's new secretary of the interior, Richard Ballinger. And Taft exacerbated the conflict through his legalistic insistence on viewing it in constitutional rather than political terms.

Taft's appointment of Ballinger, a former state judge and mayor of Seattle, was part of his judicial approach to conservation policy. Ballinger believed that Roosevelt's executive orders withdrawing land without congressional approval were illegal, and he began to restore some of the lands for private development.[10] Taft agreed with Ballinger's more legalistic approach to conservation, believing, as he did, that the president could exercise only those powers that the Constitution or the law explicitly authorized.[11] Pinchot suspected Ballinger, with some cause, as being overly sympathetic to the corporate classes, and the conflict between the men exploded in August 1909 over the disposition of federal coal lands in Alaska. Pinchot insisted that the lands should be leased from the U.S. government; Ballinger maintained that they should be sold outright.

At this point, the tale becomes intricate. A corporate syndicate known as the Clarence Cunningham group (which may have been a front for mining companies owned by the monopolists Morgan and Guggenheim) had submitted claims on the land. The General Land Office at first rejected these claims but then accepted them.[12] With Pinchot's encouragement, Louis R. Glavis, the young chief of the Portland, Oregon, division of the General Land Office, accused Ballinger of laboring under a conflict of interest when he decided to sell off the lands to the Cunningham syndicate. In 1907, when he was head of the General Land Office, Ballinger had shut down Glavis's investigation into the partnership between Cunningham and the Morgan-Guggenheim Alaska syndicate, which was seeking to develop Alaskan coal. Ballinger then went into private law practice in Seattle, where he earned a modest fee of $250 for providing legal advice to the Cunningham syndicate for an unrelated land office dispute.[13] In Glavis's view, Ballinger, who had been on the Cunningham group's payroll, had shut down his investigation to favor the financial interests of his former patrons, who had also been contributors to Taft's presidential campaign.

Pinchot arranged for Glavis to lay his charges directly before the president. On August 18, Glavis arrived at the summer White House in Beverly bearing a letter from Pinchot supporting his account. Taft reviewed the charges like a judge rather than a politician, reading Glavis's fifty-page report and consulting the attorney general.[14] He also asked Ballinger for a formal response. Ballinger set out for Beverly with Oscar Lawler, a young assistant, and on September 6 they consulted with Taft.[15] Taft was already disposed against Pinchot—he had angrily declared the day before, so loudly that everyone in the house could hear him, that "Pinchot is a fanatic and has no knowledge of discipline or interdepartmental etiquette," adding that he would "not stand for such insubordination."[16] As Taft was conducting his meeting with Ballinger and Lawler, Archie Butt predicted that the president, who "is not-overindulgent toward reformers," would uphold Ballinger and fire Pinchot, which would in turn alienate Roosevelt and array against Taft "all that set of men who look upon themselves as purists in politics."[17] That is precisely what happened.

Treating Lawler as the equivalent of his own law clerk, Taft asked him to write a memorandum "as if he were President."[18] After reviewing Lawler's memo, Taft concluded that Ballinger was innocent of fraud or any other wrongdoing. Displaying the Manichean demand for loyalty that sometimes clouded his otherwise judicial perspective, he released a letter on September 13 exonerating Ballinger of all charges. An editorial commented that Taft's letter characteristically "exhibits . . . the judicial tone and temper of a magistrate disposing of a case."[19] In a fit of anger that would prove politically unfortunate, however, Taft also fired Glavis for insubordination.[20] This was the Taft who had once assaulted a man for insulting his father—a great "hater," as Theodore Roosevelt once called him—whose obsession with personal loyalty could sometimes overcome his otherwise keen devotion to the rule of law.

Taft insisted that the firing of Glavis was necessary to maintain the administrative discipline that he considered indispensable to an efficient executive branch. "The heads of the Departments are the persons through whom I must act, and unless the bureau chiefs are subordinate to the heads it makes government of an efficient character impossible,"[21] he wrote to Nellie during his speaking tour in Oregon in early October. He predicted to Nellie that Pinchot, with his "fanaticism," was behind the controversy and was perhaps planning a "coup," and that Taft would one day have to fire him, too.[22] Meanwhile, in public speeches, Taft insisted that conservation efforts could be put on solid constitutional footing.[23] Taft wrote to Pinchot asking him to remain in government,[24] but in a separate letter to Representative William Kent, a progressive Republican, Taft insisted, "We have a government of limited power under the Constitution, and we have got to work out our problems on the basis of law. Now, if that is reactionary, then I am a reactionary."[25] At the same time, the thin-skinned president refused to take responsibility for the political firestorm he had created by firing Glavis. In November he told Archie Butt on the golf course, "I have done nothing that I would not do over again, and therefore I must feel that [the] troubles are either imaginary or else someone else is to blame."[26]

The president then asked Attorney General Wickersham to prepare a memo explaining why Taft had exonerated Ballinger. In what would prove to be the most scandalous decision of his presidency, Taft asked Wickersham to backdate the memo to September 11—the date of the attorney general's initial meeting with the president, to make it appear as though Taft had relied on the full written memo, rather than Wickersham's more cursory notes on the evidence, before making his decision.[27] But Glavis, convinced of his virtue, would not be silenced. In November he published an explosive article in *Collier's Weekly* entitled "The Whitewashing of Ballinger." "Are the Guggenheims in charge of the Department of the Interior?"[28] he asked in the article, alleging corruption without providing evidence.[29] Finally, at

Ballinger's request, Taft agreed to a congressional investigation, in the vain hope of preserving the unity of the Republican Party.[30]

Because the self-regarding Pinchot was determined to turn himself into a martyr, the investigation into the Pinchot-Ballinger affair, which riveted Washington from January through May 1910,[31] had the opposite effect. As Archie Butt reported the previous November, "I know the President does not want to force Pinchot to resign, yet he will not tolerate insubordination, much less criticism of himself."[32] As late as December 31, when Taft's brother Charlie urged him at a family wedding to fire Pinchot, Taft responded, "I am beginning to think that is just what he wants to force me to do, and I will not do it," because he was determined to avoid the "open rupture" with Roosevelt that the firing would ensure.[33]

On January 6, however, Pinchot forced Taft's hand. In anticipation of the hearings, the moralistic gadfly wrote to Senator Jonathan Dolliver of Iowa, a leader of the progressive insurgent Republicans, alleging that Taft had fired Glavis without understanding the facts.[34] The letter was read into the *Congressional Record*; the next day, Taft, always prickly on questions of honor and administrative discipline, fired Pinchot for insubordination.[35] He reached the decision after agonizing about its political consequences—"he looked like a man almost ill," Butt wrote on January 7, as Taft was making his decision. "He is weighing Pinchot in the balance but is weighing also the consequences of his own act with Roosevelt."[36]

Taft objected to Pinchot's personal disloyalty and lack of constitutional scruples, not to his conservationist zeal; to prove the point, he replaced Pinchot with another nationally acclaimed conservationist, Henry S. Graves, the head of the Yale School of Forestry, which Pinchot himself had founded. And on January 14, he issued a special message urging Congress to pass laws "to validate the withdrawals which have been made by the Secretary of the Interior and the President."[37] But the political firestorm continued: *Collier's* published a sensational follow-up attack on Ballinger, accusing him of shutting down Glavis's investigation to help Taft's election at the behest of big donors and excoriating the secretary of the interior for issuing an executive order to prevent leaks by forbidding Interior Department staffers from testifying before Congress without his approval. "Can This Be Whitewashed Also?" asked the *San Francisco Call*. "How Campaign Funds Figured—Administration Badly Tied Up."[38]

In the end, the Republican Congress exonerated Ballinger, finding no clear evidence of illegality.[39] But the hearings themselves produced a smoking gun that would indelibly define Taft's presidency. In an effort to defend Pinchot and Glavis with zeal, *Collier's* hired as counsel the crusading "People's Attorney," Louis D. Brandeis, who would go on to achieve distinction as a justice of the U.S. Supreme Court. The Pinchot-Ballinger hearings made Brandeis's national reputation as a foe of corruption. The dramatic climax of the hearings occurred when Brandeis, in his cross-examination of Ballinger and others, revealed that Wickersham had backdated his report to give the impression that Taft had relied on all the evidence before making his decision to exonerate Ballinger. Wickersham and Taft made the injury worse by initially denying the backdating before coming clean. Brandeis's smoking gun gave the impression that, instead of relying on Wickersham's memo, Taft had exonerated Ballinger based on a one-sided memo written by Lawler, Ballinger's own clerk, and then adopted Lawler's words as his own.[40]

Taft, who was always defensive in the face of criticism, first insisted that he had written the exonerating letter himself but then confessed that he indeed had relied on part of Lawler's memo,[41] telling a reporter that "he had just plain forgotten all about the memorandum."[42] The press and the public were outraged by the president's apparent deception, and although Congress ultimately exonerated him of wrongdoing, the political damage was indelible. *Hampton's Magazine* melodramatically called the Pinchot-Ballinger affair "the gravest demonstration of moral dereliction."[43]

Why did Taft tell Wickersham to backdate the memo? For such a scrupulously honest public servant, the decision seems out of character. And yet Taft's decision becomes more intelligible when viewed from his own perspective. As Taft explained in a letter to Senator Knute Nelson, the head of the investigation, he felt that changing the date would more accurately reflect the deliberative process by which he had reached his verdict.[44] Taft wrote that he had closely reviewed Glavis's charges and Ballinger's answer, as well as the attorney general's notes on the evidence, before making up his mind. Because Taft was staying up late writing constitutional orations for his upcoming fall speaking tour, he asked Lawler to prepare a memo supporting his findings. As Taft wrote to Nelson: "During the days I examined the draft opinion of Mr. Lawler, but its thirty pages did not state the case in the way I wished it stated." Taft considered the criticism of Pinchot and Glavis inappropriate and so "only used a few paragraphs from it containing merely general statements."[45]

His conclusions, Taft said, "were based upon my reading of the record, and were fortified by the oral analysis of the evidence and the conclusions which the attorney general gave me, using the notes which he had made during his reading of the record." Because he wasn't able to incorporate all of Wickersham's notes into his memo in time, he asked the attorney general to write a memo and backdate it to provide a more chronological account of the evidence on which Taft reached his conclusions. Taft further explained:

> I was very sorry not to be able to embody this analysis in my opinion, but time did not permit. I therefore directed him to embody in a written statement such analysis and conclusions as he had given me, file it with the record and date it prior to the date of my opinion, so as to show that

my decision was fortified by his summary of the evidence
and his conclusions therefrom.[46]

By backdating the memo, in other words, Taft insisted he was
being more precise rather than less in providing a chronologically
accurate trial record, including a full account of the reasons, supported by the attorney general's notes on the evidence, which he
had reviewed before reaching what he viewed as a judicial decision.

Plausible or not, Taft's explanation was good enough for
Congress. After comparing Taft's letter with Lawler's memo, the
committee concluded that Taft had indeed "studied the answers
and record, formed his own conclusions, and wrote or dictated
his own opinion, and, as a matter of fact, did not adopt the Lawler
memorandum."[47] And at least some journalists accepted the
explanation as well. The *National Tribune* observed that backdating documents was common government practice.[48] The *Chicago
Record-Herald* suggested there was "absolutely nothing wrong in
in instructing a subordinate to prepare an opinion."[49] But progressive publications such as *Collier's*, *McClure's*, and *Outlook* excori-
ated Taft. Acting more like a vindictive politician than a judge,
the president uncharacteristically—and unsuccessfully—tried to
retaliate by asking Congress to raise the postal rates on national
magazines; he argued that the government shouldn't subsidize
journalists who were failing in their duty to "occupy a disin-
terred position" as "controllers of public opinion."[50] These clumsy
attempts to punish the press led, predictably and appropriately,
to even more vigorous reproach.

Taft's sin, then, was not obstruction of justice (beyond his
initial denial, which was not under oath and which he eventually
recanted) but a tendency to surround himself with loyalists and
to lash out against those he viewed as disloyal. Taft could have
avoided the scandal by admitting that he had backdated the
memo and by accepting Ballinger's repeatedly proffered resigna-

tion.[51] Instead, he compounded his error by expressing unequivocal support for his secretary of the interior,[52] perhaps because the judicially minded president always felt most comfortable resisting the approval of the crowd. In Taft's mind, political unpopularity was a tribute to his devotion to principle, a measure of success rather than failure. It was in March 1910 that he memorably declared to Archie Butt, "I will not play a part for popularity."[53]

Whether principled or blinkered, Taft's decision to stand by Ballinger and to throw over Pinchot led to a serious breach with Theodore Roosevelt. In April, as the Ballinger hearings were boiling over, Pinchot took a steamship to the French Riviera to meet with Roosevelt, who had just returned from a long safari in Africa. The two men concluded that Taft had betrayed Roosevelt's legacy by failing to protect the environment, enforce antitrust laws, and lower the tariffs—all charges that proved to be inaccurate. Roosevelt then wrote to Senator Henry Cabot Lodge of Massachusetts, his longtime ally, to complain that Taft had "completely twisted round the policies I advocated and acted upon."[54] As a result, the former president wrote, he could not support the administration in the upcoming congressional elections. After a year of silence, Taft wrote to Roosevelt in May, flagellating himself for his political failures. "It is now a year and three months since I assumed office and I have had a hard time," Taft wrote dolefully. "I do not know that I have had harder luck than other Presidents, but I do know that thus far I have succeeded far less than have others. I have been conscientiously trying to carry out your policies, but my method for doing so has not worked smoothly."[55]

Instead of explaining his decisions about Pinchot and Ballinger, he told Roosevelt—as he had earlier told Congress when proposing tariff reductions—that the former president should simply read his public statements and "look into that wholly for yourself."[56] Taft invited Roosevelt to the White House to heal the growing breach, but Roosevelt declined on the unconvincing grounds that, as Archie Butt reported, "he was opposed to the idea of ex-Presidents visiting Washington."[57] Taft later learned that Roosevelt had been offended by his assurances, in the letter of invitation, that he would never forget what his brother Charlie and Roosevelt had done for him in the 1908 campaign; Roosevelt thought he alone deserved the credit for Taft's nomination.[58]

Tensions between the president and his predecessor escalated in the summer of 1910, when Roosevelt opposed Secretary Ballinger's campaign for a U.S. Senate seat in Washington State. When Nellie Taft learned of Roosevelt's decision, she observed presciently to the president, "Well, I suppose you will have to fight Mr. Roosevelt for the nomination [in 1912], and if you get it he will defeat you."[59] In August, during a party leadership contest in New York, a candidate supported by Vice President James Sherman defeated one supported by Roosevelt, who suspected Taft of conspiring to humiliate him. "What awful politics!" Butt confided to his diary, writing that Taft and Sherman were "like a lot of children at the game when compared to Mr. Roosevelt."[60] He also observed that Taft's scheming secretary Charles Norton was goading Roosevelt into challenging Taft for the presidency.

Roosevelt took the bait. He set out west for a three-week speaking tour during which he attacked the Supreme Court as a barrier to progressive legislation and endorsed popular checks on the ability of judges to overturn laws. (Taft was so distressed at these attacks that he hurled a golf club in frustration.)[61] On August 31, in Osawatomie, Kansas, Roosevelt delivered his radical "New Nationalism" speech. "This New Nationalism regards the executive power as the steward of the public welfare," Roosevelt declared. "It demands of the judiciary that it shall be interested primarily in human welfare rather than in property, just as it demands that the representative body shall represent all the people rather than any one class or section of the people."[62]

As many Republicans feared, the 1910 midterm elections were a stinging rebuke of Taft and conservatism, and the Democrats took control of the House of Representatives for the first time since 1894, although the Republicans retained their majority in the Senate. Stung by the defeat, which he viewed as a personal repudiation by Republican progressives, Taft turned for solace to an alliance with the standpat Republicans in Congress.

Although Roosevelt and his allies believed that Taft had betrayed Roosevelt's record on tariff reform, conservation, and antitrust prosecutions, Taft's achievements in all three areas arguably surpassed Roosevelt's own. Taft's dramatic ramping up of antitrust prosecutions was the most visible example of his success. Taft and Roosevelt had different approaches to antitrust, reflecting their different views of the Constitution. Roosevelt championed big government as well as big business: he wanted to create a federal bureau of corporations to regulate trusts, prosecuting the bad ones (whose predatory behavior harmed competition), while supporting the good ones (whose economies of scale helped consumers). The most significant example of this Jesuitical distinction between good and bad trusts had been Roosevelt's decision as president to bring an antitrust suit against the Northern Securities railroad trust, controlled by J. P. Morgan, but not against U.S. Steel, which Morgan also controlled.

Taft, by contrast, believed in vigorous and consistent enforcement of the Sherman Antitrust Act, and his decision to prosecute U.S. Steel would deliver the coup de grâce to his fraying relationship with Roosevelt. Denouncing monopolies during the 1908 campaign in Sandusky, Ohio, Taft had promised even more vigorous enforcement of the antitrust law than Roosevelt, to prevent the formation of monopolies in the first place.[63] The trusts stifled competition, he said, by allowing "the aggregation of wealth in plants so great the owners of it were able, by cunningly devised means, to stifle competition, to control prices of goods and shove them up above what the cost of production would justify."[64] To combat these economic wiles, Taft declared, "What we need is to increase the machinery of government, to increase the supervision of these combinations that have the temptation to violate the law . . . so that these prosecutions can be carried on with great rapidity."[65]

As president, Taft made good on his promise. In an address to Congress on January 7, 1910, Taft made the case for the Mann-Elkins Act, drafted by Attorney General Wickersham, which increased the powers of the Interstate Commerce Commission to control the rates charged by railroads and telegraph and telephone companies.[66] In his comprehensive and legalistic speech, Taft talked about the need for speedy and uniform review of challenges to railroad rates and also recommended establishing a five-member "United States Court of Commerce."[67] Congress responded enthusiastically to his recommendations and, five months later, passed the Mann-Elkins Act, which Taft promptly signed.

In his speech to Congress, Taft also gave an extended explanation of his view of antitrust law, emphasizing that the government should focus not on the size of the enterprise but rather on the "aggregation of capital and plants with the express or implied intent to restrain interstate or foreign commerce, or to monopolize it in whole or in part."[68] As he had done since his days on the bench, Taft insisted that the illegality of actions by trusts or unions turned on malicious intent, not simply on size.[69]

Taft criticized the Sugar Trust case, *United States v. E.C. Knight Co.* (1895),[70] where the Court upheld the constitutionality of the Sherman antitrust law but ruled that it did not apply to manufacturing, since manufacturing could not be equated with interstate commerce.[71] Taft also implicitly criticized Justice Holmes's suggestion in the *Northern Securities* case that the Sherman Act should be read to forbid not all restraints of trade, but only those that the Court decided were unreasonable. The judicial effort to ban only unreasonable restraints of trade, Taft declared, would "put into the hands of the court a power impossible to exercise on any consistent principle . . . to give them a power approaching the arbitrary, the abuse of which might involve our whole judicial system in disaster."[72]

After his speech, Taft anxiously awaited the Court's pending decision in the *Standard Oil* case, originally brought by the Roosevelt administration. The suit alleged that Standard Oil of New Jersey, the parent company of John D. Rockefeller's many-headed hydra, had monopolized the oil refining and shipping trades.[73] The Supreme Court finally heard the case in March 1910 but didn't issue its decision for more than a year. Taft fretted that the delay was postponing Congress's consideration of his proposal to pass a national incorporation act.[74] Finally, on May 15, 1911, the Court handed down its decision.[75] Chief Justice Edward White adopted the very argument that Taft had repeatedly criticized— namely, that the Sherman Act should be construed in light of the "rule of reason," prohibiting only unreasonable restraints of trade. Despite its weakening of the Sherman Act, which does not mention the word "reasonable," the Court ruled against Rockefeller and ordered the Standard Oil Trust to divest about thirty of its subsidiaries. Although the Court's reasoning contradicted his own, Taft was happy enough with the result to exclaim, when he heard it, "Bully for that!"[76]

Taft's friend Justice John Marshall Harlan criticized the reasoning of the *Standard Oil* decision along lines similar to those that Taft himself had sketched out to Congress. Harlan cited a Senate report declining to amend the Sherman Act to include the rule of reason on the ground that the amendment would "entirely emasculate" the bill because "the injection of the rule of reasonableness or unreasonableness would lead to the greatest variableness and uncertainty in the enforcement of the law."[77]

Two weeks later, on May 29, the Court handed down another important decision, in the case against the Tobacco Trust. The Court, with Chief Justice White once again applying the rule of reason, held that the trust was illegal because of the clear intentions of its corporate founders "to monopolize the trade by driving competitors out of business, which were ruthlessly carried out upon the assumption that to work upon the fears or play upon the cupidity of competitors would make success possible."[78] Justice Harlan again dissented in part, on the ground that the Court had rewritten the Sherman Act and refused to break up the trust, instead sending the hydra back to the lower court for its tender disposition.

President Taft's devotion to defending the institutional legitimacy of the Court always overcame his devotion to his own constitutional interpretations. He praised the *Standard Oil* opinion as a "good opinion—the Standard Oil Company will have to dissolve," even as he confessed that the reasoning of the Court "did not take exactly the line of distinction I have drawn, but it certainly approximates it."[79] And he praised the Tobacco Trust decision with similar casuistry, insisting that there was "no conflict between what I have said and what the court says," instead detecting "a real resemblance between them that makes me proud." Although he had previously suggested the opposite, the president now declared that the Court's decision to read the "rule of reason" into the Sherman Act did not, in fact, permit it to distinguish between "good" and "bad" trusts.[80] For the judicial president, defending the integrity of the Court was more important than pressing his own views.

Later that year, Taft's judicial frame of mind led him to make the most legally principled and politically unwise decision of his presidency. On October 26, 1911, his administration filed an antitrust suit against U.S. Steel, the first billion-dollar corporation in the world.[81] It had been created by the merger of nearly a dozen steel companies controlled by J. P. Morgan, Andrew Carnegie, and other titans, and it produced one-quarter of the world's steel.[82] The Justice Department charged that the monopolistic powers of the Steel Trust had been increased during the Panic of

1907, when it acquired the Tennessee Coal and Iron Company with President Roosevelt's blessing. The suggestion was that the acquisition, at what turned out to be a bargain price, threatened competition rather than saving the economy, and that Roosevelt had been duped by J. P. Morgan.[83] The headlines the next day proclaimed "Roosevelt Fooled."[84]

Roosevelt, furious and defensive, insisted that he had not been misled in allowing the Steel Trust to buy the Tennessee Coal Company,[85] stating forcefully that Morgan had told the truth about the need to buy the company to rescue the economy. He added that Taft, as a member of his cabinet, had reviewed the merger and "was enthusiastic in his praise of what was done."[86] But Roosevelt had indeed been duped in 1907, misunderstanding the complicated financial facts in a well-intentioned effort to stave off the panic.[87] Taft insisted that he hadn't known about the suit before the Justice Department filed it, but in Roosevelt's eyes, Taft's ignorance made his disloyalty all the worse. Roosevelt's sister Corinne Roosevelt Robinson told Archie Butt in January 1912 that her brother "could never forgive" the president for filing the steel suit.[88]

He didn't. Roosevelt wrote an article for *Outlook* magazine arguing that Taft's trust-busting agenda was too aggressive and that the president was wrongly focused on breaking up corporations through lawsuits rather than subjecting their unfair practices to vigorous regulation under an expanded bureau of corporations. The only way to prevent unfair competition, Roosevelt declared, "is by strict Government supervision, and not merely by lawsuits." He accused Taft and others who relied exclusively on antitrust enforcement of calling themselves progressives by representing "in reality in this matter not progress at all but a kind of sincere rural toryism," which would return American business to the eighteenth century. Roosevelt ended with a clarion call for regulating successful trusts rather than breaking them up. "It is practically impossible . . . to try to break up all combinations merely because they are large and successful," he declared.[89]

This article spurred rumors that Roosevelt would challenge Taft in the 1912 election. The *New York World* asked, "Has Theodore Roosevelt Now Become Mr. Morgan's Candidate for President?" And Roosevelt himself later credited this article with "bringing me forward for the Presidential nomination."[90] Years later, in 1920, the Supreme Court would rule that U.S. Steel did not constitute an unlawful monopoly under the Sherman Act, but by that point the political damage had been done.

On December 5, 1911, Taft delivered his annual message to Congress, discussing at length and in legalistic detail the recent Supreme Court decisions dissolving the Standard Oil and American Tobacco trusts. The president noted with approval that the government had been working for more than twenty years to make the antitrust statute effective, "and only in the last three or four years has the heavy hand of the law been laid upon the great illegal combinations that have exercised such an absolute dominion over many of our industries."[91] Defending himself against Roosevelt's charge that he was antibusiness, Taft insisted that the Sherman Act applied to the accumulation of "large capital in business enterprises" only when its purpose was to "stifle competition." Taft added, "Mere size is no sin against the law."[92]

A month earlier, an editorial in the New York *Journal of Commerce* concluded, "President Taft has not been as loud or spectacular in his attacks upon the 'trusts' as was his predecessor in the White House, but he has been consistent, persistent, and unwavering and results have been achieved or at any rate have culminated during his administration that have been distressing to Wall Street."[93] And as the election of 1912 approached, Taft called his antitrust program "firm, consistent and effective," noting that Roosevelt had brought forty-four antitrust cases in nearly eight years as president while his own administration had brought almost seventy cases in less than four years.[94]

Foreign policy was the final area where Taft attempted valiantly, but not always successfully, to put Roosevelt's legacy on firm constitutional ground. Unlike Roosevelt, he was scrupulous about seeking congressional approval for his foreign interventions, noting accurately that the Constitution gives Congress, not the president, the power to declare war. Taft's foreign policy was based on the promotion of what others called "dollar diplomacy" and what Taft called the substitution of "dollars for bullets."[95] He insisted that diplomacy should be guided by "the increase of trade relations and commerce," rather than the unilateral use of force. As Taft put it, he and Secretary of State Philander Knox, who had been Roosevelt's attorney general, believed that foreign policy "may be well made to include active intervention to secure for our merchandise and our capitalists opportunity for profitable investment which shall insure to the benefit of both countries concerned."[96]

The most vivid constitutional drama involving Taft's dollar diplomacy arose over Mexico. In March 1911, without consulting his cabinet, Taft mobilized twenty thousand American troops along the Mexican border to protect Americans in Mexico in the face of uprisings against President Porfirio Díaz.[97] Taft worried that billions of dollars of American capital invested in Mexico might be at risk.[98] But although the Mexican government expected an invasion, Taft was careful to instruct his commanders not to cross the Mexican border without first seeking congressional approval, believing that he lacked the authority as commander in chief to act unilaterally. In the event, as Taft expected, Congress refused to authorize the troops to cross the border, and Taft kept them mobilized as a deterrent without starting a war.

Taft also deserves credit for putting constitutional principles above party. When he read a dispatch in May reporting that four Americans had been killed in Mexico, and his wife asked if there would be war, Taft replied, "I only know that I am going to do everything in my power to prevent one. Already there is a movement in the Grand Old Party"—he intoned the words sarcastically—"to utilize this trouble for party ends. . . . I am afraid I am a constant disappointment to my party. The fact of the matter is, the longer I am President the less of a party man I seem to become. . . . [I]t seems to me to be impossible to be a strict party man and serve the whole country impartially."[99] Still, bucking the popular cry for war took its toll. During a White House reception in August 1911, after confiding to Archie Butt that he was being pressured to declare war, the president "broke down and wept as I have never seen anyone weep in my life," as Butt recalled. "His whole body was shaken with convulsive sobs."[100]

In his December 1911 address to Congress, Taft explained his constitutionally scrupulous position: "It seems my duty as Commander in Chief to place troops in sufficient number where, if Congress shall direct that they enter Mexico to save American lives and property, an effective movement may be promptly made."[101] But Taft emphasized that he would not act unilaterally. "The assumption by the press that I contemplate intervention on Mexican soil to protect American lives or property is of course gratuitous, because I seriously doubt whether I have such authority under any circumstances, and if I had I would not exercise it without express congressional approval."[102] An unauthorized invasion, he suggested, might create further bloodshed without dampening the fires of revolution.[103] In the end, the Mexican turmoil continued long after Taft left the presidency.[104]

In the wake of Taft's statement, Roosevelt criticized the president for lack of leadership in foreign affairs. After leaving office, Taft joked wanly that Roosevelt divided presidents into "Lincoln Presidents" and "Buchanan Presidents," alluding to the weak chief executive who took no action to prevent the Southern states from seceding in the winter of 1860–61. (In another example of presidential deference, Buchanan asked Congress to approve his request to deploy troops to Central America; when Congress refused, he, like Taft, meekly submitted.)[105] Taft added that Roosevelt "places himself in the Lincoln class of Presidents, and me in the Buchanan class."[106] This reminded Taft of the story of a young girl who comes home and announces, "Papa, I am the best scholar in the class" not because her teacher told her but because "I just noticed it myself."[107] And yet Taft's constitutionally scrupulous position about the president's lack of authority to send troops on his own across the Mexican border also called to mind that of Lincoln himself. After President James K. Polk moved troops to the Mexican-American border in 1846, in response to what he claimed was the emergency of a Mexican invasion, precipitating the Mexican War, Lincoln—elected later that year as a constitutionally minded Whig congressman from Illinois—introduced his famous "spot" resolutions, demanding that Polk identify the precise spot where blood had been shed, to prove it was on U.S. soil.[108] (The resolutions earned him the nickname "Spotty Lincoln.")

Taft and Knox believed that free trade and dollar diplomacy within a clear legal framework would help the American economy by expanding markets for American exports in Latin America and the Far East.[109] His maxim: speak softly and carry a free trade agreement. Although the success of dollar diplomacy was mixed, Taft proved to be a visionary in attempting to create treaties and intergovernmental organizations to promote free trade. His most ambitious initiative was his crusade for a free trade treaty between Canada and the United States, known in the jargon of the day as the Canadian Tariff Reciprocity Agreement. The goal was to apply the minimum rates of the Payne-Aldrich tariff to all trade with Canada.[110] On January 26, 1911, Taft sent a special message to Congress urging it to pass the Canadian free trade treaty as soon as possible. Taft praised Canada as a diplomatic ally and an expanding market for American goods: "She has cost us nothing in the way of preparations for defense against her possible assault, and she never will. . . . I therefore earnestly hope that the measure will be promptly enacted into law."[111]

It wasn't. Congress refused to act, and Taft threatened to call the House and Senate back for an extra session. On March 4, he made good on his threat.[112] A month later, on April 5, Taft, who communicated to Congress with proclamations rather than cajoleries, sent another special message. "I felt assured that the sentiment of the people of the United States was such that they would welcome a measure which would result in the increase of trade on both sides of the boundary line," he declared.[113] He later told a wavering senator, "I regard this as the most important measure of my administration . . . I am striving to bring about what I think will be an epoch in our country's history."[114] On April 21, the House finally approved the bill, and the Senate followed on July 22. "It was passed by a vote of about two to one, but largely by Democratic votes," Archie Butt recorded, adding that Taft "was very much pleased, but would have felt much better had more Republicans voted for the measure."[115] The president signed the Canadian Tariff Reciprocity Agreement on July 26, 1911; the historian David H. Burton has called it the "most significant legislative victory of the Sixty-second Congress," and perhaps of Taft's entire presidency.[116]

Alas, Taft, who had a habit of shooting himself in the foot, had written a letter to Roosevelt in January predicting that "the amount of Canadian products that we would take could produce a current of business between western Canada and the United States that would make Canada only an adjunct to the United States."[117] Taft's letter was leaked to the press and the resulting uproar led the Canadian people, in a Brexit-style referendum, to reject the treaty on September 21, 1911. The new Canadian prime minister, a conservative populist, lashed out against the U.S. president as "tricky Taft."[118] Taft was crushed by the defeat of what he viewed as sound policy, but he was indifferent, as always, to the political fallout. In a handwritten postscript to a letter to his brother Horace, he wrote, "I am sorry about reciprocity on account of the real loss to both countries and its defeat. Its political effect I can't calculate and I don't care about."[119]

Perhaps the most vivid example of Taft's judicial approach to foreign policy was his dream of setting up what he called in his 1911 message to Congress "an interlacing and interlocking series of treaties comprehending so many countries as to lead to the formation of an international court of judicature."[120] Taft first took up the cause of creating a world court in February 1910, when he accepted the post of honorary president of the newly formed American Society for the Judicial Settlement of International Disputes.[121] "I don't see any more reason why matters of national honor should not be referred to a court," he remarked, ". . . any more than matters of property or matters of national proprietorship."[122] Taft believed that only a court with the jurisdiction to arbitrate "all questions" giving rise to international disputes, including questions of national honor—that is, vital interests like immigration policy or the Monroe Doctrine—could end war and promote world peace. Taft and Secretary of State Knox persuaded the French and British ambassadors to the United States to sign arbitration treaties that called for "unlimited arbitration" of all international disputes.[123] But Taft failed to consult with any senators, including those on the Foreign Relations Committee. Following the lead of Roosevelt, who insisted that "the United States should never bind itself to arbitrate questions respecting its honor, independence, and integrity," the Senate in August eviscerated Taft's proposal for unlimited arbitration treaties with Britain and France by deleting a paragraph that would have referred all international arbitration questions to an international court.[124]

Taft's speeches on behalf of the treaties led to his final breach with Roosevelt. On a western tour stumping for ratification of the treaties in the fall of 1911, Taft struggled to connect with audiences. Archie Butt reported in October, "He gives too much detail and not enough general principles, but he will not say things he does not believe."[125] In that spirit of compulsive honesty, Taft declared, "I think that war might have been settled without a fight and ought to have been. So with the Mexican War. So, I think, with the Spanish war."[126] These were, understandably, fighting words to a bellicose former president who had found glory on the battlefields of Cuba in 1898, and on December 26 Roosevelt refused to attend a peace banquet where Taft made the case for the arbitration treaties. The Colonel, as Roosevelt then liked to be known, proceeded to denounce the treaties in *Outlook*.

Roosevelt's attack wounded Taft more than any other; he told Archie Butt that "it is hard, very hard, Archie, to see a devoted friendship going to pieces like a rope of sand."[127] The treaties went to pieces as well. In March 1912, the Senate amended the treaties and passed them with significant reservations, excluding from the arbitration court any disputes over the admission of aliens to the United States or to U.S. public schools, as well as any disputes arising under the Monroe Doctrine.[128]

Because of the nativist clauses singling out aliens, among other provisions, Taft considered the revised arbitration treaties fatally flawed and refused to forward them to Britain and France. Taft was strikingly opposed to discrimination against aliens: he vetoed a bill that would have required a literacy test for immigrants.[129] And Taft also opposed California's ultimately successful efforts to discriminate against Japanese aliens.[130] (Roosevelt responded in his autobiography that Taft had been wrong and that the United States should be free to exclude any group of aliens it pleased.)[131]

But despite the failure of his free trade and arbitration treaties, and his idealistic dream of a world court, Taft's vision was the beginning of our modern system of international arbitration—a web of bilateral and multilateral treaties from the International Criminal Court to the North American Free Trade Agreement and the World Trade Organization. Years later, recalling the Senate's emasculation of the treaties, Taft chuckled as he acknowledged that they would have done little to promote world peace in their diminished form: "So I put them on the shelf, and let the dust accumulate on them in the hope that the senators might change their minds, or that the people might change the Senate; instead of which they changed me."[132]

5

"Popular Unrest":
The Election of 1912 and the
Battle for the Constitution

On February 21, 1912, after delivering a speech called "A Char-ter for Democracy" at the Ohio Constitutional Convention in Columbus, Theodore Roosevelt made the decision to challenge William Howard Taft for the Republican nomination for presi-dent. The speech, a radical attack on judicial independence and on constitutional checks on the passions of the people, defined the election in Taft's mind as a crusade to defend the Constitution and the rule of law against the pure democracy threatened by Roosevelt, who was increasingly sounding like a demagogue.

"I believe in pure democracy," Roosevelt began. "It is a prime duty of the people to free our government from the control of money in politics," he continued, and "unless representative gov-ernment does absolutely represent the people it is not represen-tative government at all." As a result, he demanded, "as weapons in the hands of the people, all governmental devices which will make the representatives of the people more easily and certainly responsible to the people's will." Roosevelt endorsed a series of populist reforms, including elected state judiciaries, presidential primaries based on "direct nominations by the people," and direct election of U.S. senators, adding, "I believe in the initiative and the referendum, which should be used not to destroy representative government, but to correct it when ever it becomes misrepresentative."[1]

What most alarmed Taft and other constitutionalists was Roosevelt's attack on judicial independence. He assailed Supreme Court justice William Moody by name for ruling against "a railway man named Howard, I think." The former president sounded most radical when he endorsed the right of the people to overturn state court decisions they thought incorrect or to recall state judges with whom they disagreed. "When a judge decides a constitutional question, when he decides what the people as a whole can or cannot do, the people should have the right to recall that decision if they think it wrong," Roosevelt declared.[2]

In the Cleveland train station, on the way back from Columbus, Roosevelt announced his candidacy for president. "My hat is in the ring," he said. "The fight is on and I am stripped to the buff." Days later, he distributed a letter from eleven Republican governors asking him to challenge Taft, along with his reply: "I will accept the nomination for President if it is tendered to me, and I will adhere to this decision until the convention has expressed its preference."[3] That evening, before a White House dinner, Taft was handed an Associated Press report on Roosevelt's statement, which he read and passed along to his guests.

"I told you so four years ago, and you would not believe me," Nellie exclaimed, breaking the silence.

"I know you did, my dear, and I think you are perfectly happy now," Taft replied. "You would have preferred the Colonel to come out against me than to have been wrong yourself."[4]

Although Taft believed that Roosevelt would beat him at the Republican Convention in June, he was roused to fight on behalf

of the cause he cared most passionately about: preserving
judicial independence and the Constitution. On April 25, during a long address in Boston, Taft declared that "the charter of
democracy" Roosevelt proposed in Ohio "advocated a change in
our judicial system" that "would be dangerous to the body politic."
The recall of judges and their decisions, he said, "would necessarily destroy the keystone of our liberties by taking away judicial independence, and by exposing to the chance of one popular
vote, questions of the continuance of our constitutional guarantees of life, liberty and property and the pursuit of happiness."[5]
If only his own ambition were at stake, Taft said, he would ignore
Roosevelt's charges that he was under the thumb of "an aristoc-
racy of party bosses," but "I represent a cause" and "the cause is
that of progress of the people in pursuit of happiness under
constitutional government."[6] Taft answered eleven of Roosevelt's charges (numbered as in a legal brief!), ranging from
"unfair charges as to bosses" to "repudiates his own trust record."
He then concluded his address with a passionate defense of judicial
independence.

> One who so lightly regards constitutional principles, and
> especially, the independence of the judiciary, one who is
> so naturally impatient of legal restraints, and of due legal
> procedure, and who has so misunderstood what liberty
> regulated by law is, could not be safely intrusted with suc-
> cessive presidential terms. I say this sorrowfully, but I say
> it with the full conviction of truth.[7]

After unburdening himself of this fervent address, Taft retired
to the presidential railroad car, where a journalist found him with
his head in his hands. "Roosevelt was my closest friend," he
exclaimed, looking up with anguish. And then he began to weep.[8]
Behind the scenes, though, Taft was undaunted. He worked

with Republican political bosses to secure his renomination through the various state conventions rather than relying on the handful of direct primaries. Six states in the North and West held primaries at the beginning of the election year; six more states would join them before the Republican Convention in June. Forced to submit himself to the direct consideration of the people, Taft campaigned vigorously: after winning the Massachusetts primary, he told a crowd in Maryland, "I am a man of peace and don't want to fight. But when I do fight I want to hit hard. *Even a rat in a corner will fight.*"[9] After alarming the public with this unfortunate image, he lamented the "hypocrisy, the insincerity, the selfishness, the monumental egotism, and almost the insanity of the megalomania that possess Theodore Roosevelt." Roosevelt reciprocated by calling Taft a "puzzlewit" and a "fathead"[10] as well as "a flubdub with a streak of the second-rate and the common in him."[11]

In the end, Taft won the New York and Massachusetts primaries, but lost to Roosevelt in California, Minnesota, Maryland, Nebraska, New Jersey, Ohio, Pennsylvania, and South Dakota. (Both men failed to carry their home states.) Senator Robert La Follette took North Dakota and his home state of Wisconsin. All told, in the states that held direct primaries, Roosevelt won 1,157,397 votes and 278 delegates; Taft, 761,716 votes and 48 delegates; and La Follette 351,043 and 36 delegates.[12] But 254 delegates were still contested, and the rest of the delegates would be allocated at the Republican Convention in Chicago in June. A candidate needed the votes of 504 delegates to win the nomination.

At the beginning of that month, the Republican National Committee awarded 235 of the contested seats to Taft and only 19 to Roosevelt, depriving the former president of dozens of delegates (the precise number remains disputed) to which he plausibly claimed he was entitled.[13] Days before the convention opened on June 18, Roosevelt declared, "I'm feeling like a bull moose!" and called on the credentials committee to allocate more than 70 of the additional contested seats to him rather than Taft.[14] In the Chicago Coliseum, Roosevelt gave the most melodramatic speech of his career, culminating with the messianic battle cry, "We stand at Armageddon, and we battle for the Lord."[15] In response, twenty thousand of his supporters sang "Onward, Christian Soldiers." Taft had the wit to appoint as chairman of the convention the conservative New York attorney Elihu Root, who was close to both Taft and Roosevelt. Root delivered a keynote address promising that the Republican Party would uphold the integrity of the courts and the Constitution.[16] Root then settled the matter by awarding 71 contested delegates to Taft rather than Roosevelt. This prompted Roosevelt supporters to express their conviction that their champion had been steamrolled by repeatedly exclaiming "toot toot" and "choo choo."[17] Taft was promptly nominated on the first ballot, with 561 votes to Roosevelt's 107 and La Follette's 41. Protesting the lack of progressive representation on what was now branded as a conservative ticket, 344 delegates refused to vote.[18] Roosevelt and his delegates walked out and held a rump convention of their own, where the former president exhorted his supporters to remember the commandment "Thou Shalt Not Steal."[19] The new party would soon be called the Progressive Party and was popularly known as the Bull Moose Party, after one of Roosevelt's favorite expressions.

Did party bosses loyal to Taft steal the Republican nomination from Roosevelt? Taft's biographer Henry Pringle concludes that the answer hardly matters, given the party rules in place at the time. "Whether thirty votes were stolen or seventy-two or none has no real bearing on the outcome in Chicago during those humid days of June, 1912," Pringle concludes. "The Republican party was in the hands of the forces which favored Taft's renomination."[20] Taft, for his part, criticized the direct primary, as opposed to the convention system, as encouraging the election of demagogues rather than moderates.

In July, Taft lamented to Nellie that Roosevelt "is utterly unscrupulous in his method of stating things, and his power of attracting public attention is marvelous. I think he has really convinced a great number of people of the United States that we committed gross frauds, that I am the receiver of stolen goods in taking the nomination."[21] A month later, Taft complained to his wife again, calling Roosevelt "the fakir, the juggler, the green goods man, the gold brick man that he has come to be." The president accused his predecessor of "seeking to make his followers 'Holy Rollers,' and I hope that the country is beginning to see this. . . . So far as personal relations with him are concerned, they don't exist."[22] During the campaign that followed, Taft would maintain, remarkably, that he preferred the election of Woodrow Wilson, the Democratic nominee, to the election of Roosevelt, even though he recoiled from Wilson's "general radicalism" and criticisms of the Constitution and found his acceptance speech "purring and ladylike."[23]

In his heart, Taft viewed both Roosevelt and Wilson as threats to the Constitution. Unfortunately for Taft, his attempts to defend the Constitution against assaults from both sides were drowned out by a debate that proved more galvanizing to voters: the debate between Wilson's New Freedom and Roosevelt's New Nationalism. That debate asked whether centralizing or decentralizing corporate and government power was the best way to tame the trusts and protect the economic interests of the middle classes. The Jeffersonian Wilson, guided by his economic advisor Louis Brandeis, who had denounced "the curse of bigness" in business and government, insisted on regulating competition by breaking up the banks or preventing them from consolidating in the first place. The Hamiltonian Roosevelt, influenced by

Herbert Croly, the editor of the *New Republic,* called for big regulatory bodies to oversee the big corporations.[24] And the constitutionalist Taft called for vigorous enforcement of the anti-trust laws to break up the most egregious trusts; he also defended the importance of independent courts to keep big government as well as big business within legal and constitutional bounds. In the battle between the competing visions of Roosevelt and Wilson,[25] Taft's constitutionalism struggled for attention as a countertheme to the major fugue.

All three platforms framed their programs in constitutional terms. Roosevelt's Progressive Party advocated publicity of campaign donations, minimum wage and maximum hour laws, and other reforms. "We hold with Thomas Jefferson and Abraham Lincoln that the people are the masters of their Constitution, to fulfill its purposes and to safeguard it from those who, by perversion of its intent, would convert it into an instrument of injustice," the Progressive platform declared.[26] Taft's Republican platform, by contrast, unequivocally emphasized judicial independence, declaring: "The Republican Party reaffirms its intention to uphold at all times the authority and integrity of the Courts, both State and Federal, and it will ever insist that their powers to enforce their process and to protect life, liberty and property shall be preserved inviolate."[27] As for Wilson's Democratic platform, it connected constitutional principles to economic reform. "We declare it to be a fundamental principle of the Democratic Party that the Federal government, under the Constitution, has no right or power to impose or collect tariff duties, except for the purpose of revenue."[28]

As the Democratic platform suggested, the election was also a battle over the tariff. "We favor the immediate downward revision" of "the high republican tariff," the Democrats declared, and "we denounce the action of President Taft in vetoing the bills to reduce the tariff in the cotton, woolen, metals, and chemical schedules, and the farmers' free-list bill, all of which were

designed to give immediate relief to the masses from the exac-
tions of the trusts."[29] The Republican platform countered, "We
reaffirm our belief in a protective tariff," although "some of the
existing import duties are too high, and should be reduced."[30]
And the Progressive Party essentially split the difference, endors-
ing "a protective tariff which shall equalize conditions of competition between the United States and foreign countries, both
for the farmer and the manufacturer, and which shall maintain
for labor an adequate standard of living." It also condemned "the
Payne-Aldrich bill as unjust to the people" and the Democratic
platform for being "committed to the destruction of the protective system through a tariff for revenue only, a policy which
would inevitably produce widespread industrial and commercial
disaster." With a faith in experts shared by all three candidates,
the Progressives, like the Republicans, called for "a non-partisan
scientific tariff commission, reporting both to the President and
to either branch of Congress."[31]

After winning the Republican nomination from a rival he considered an illiberal demagogue, Taft initially seemed indifferent
to winning the general election.[32] By July 22, he took on a self-
pitying tone: "The Bull Moose continues to roar as much as ever,
but I don't think he frightens as many people. Sometimes I think
I might as well give up so far as being a candidate is concerned.
There are so many people in the country who don't like me.
Without knowing much about me, they don't like me—apparently
on the Dr. Fell principle."[33] ("I do not like thee, Doctor Fell,"
went the old nursery rhyme, "The reason why—I cannot tell.")
Taft insisted defensively that he was indifferent to popular dis-
dain: "The truth is that it is not the height of my ambition to be
popular, and I have become quite philosophical with respect to
the dislike the people may feel for me, because generally I can
attribute it to some misrepresentation."[34] On July 24, he wrote
to Nellie about a trip that his son Bob and daughter Helen
were taking to Glacier National Park, and joked that they should

"enjoy all the privileges they can on this trip because they may not continue to be the son and daughter of a President for very long."[35]

Whatever his ambivalence about the campaign of 1912, Taft's constitutional passions and competitive spirit were roused in his speech on August 1 accepting the Republican nomination. His address focused on the Republican Party's commitment to defending the Founders' Constitution and on the injustices he had suffered from "a reign of sensational journalism and unjust and unprincipled muckraking."[36]

Taft then gave a comprehensive accounting of his own accomplishments. He had kept the promise of his 1908 acceptance speech, he stressed, to give "special attention to the machinery of government with a view to increasing its efficiency and decreasing its cost."[37] Citing budget figures to make the point that he had moved the government from deficit to surplus by cutting $50 million in expenses and increasing revenues with the Payne tariff and corporation tax,[38] Taft went on to say that he had reorganized government with the help of "an Economy and Efficiency Commission, consisting of the ablest experts in the country."[39] In foreign relations, "we have maintained peace everywhere and sought to promote its continuance and permanence," although he complained that the Senate had amended beyond repair his proposed "broad treaties for the promotion of universal arbitration." In Mexico, Taft said, his self-restraint in refusing to provoke war by sending troops over the border, despite populist calls for an invasion, had saved hundreds of millions of dollars and thousands of lives.

On free trade, he said, the Payne-Aldrich bill "furnished the opportunity for insisting on the removal by foreign countries of discriminations in that trade," raising America's exports and imports to "a higher figure than ever before in the history of the country." Taft said that he had kept the promises of the Republican platform of 1908 by calling a special session of Congress to reduce the tariff, and as a result "prosperity has been gradually restored since the panic of 1907." Finally, Taft said that the Supreme Court's decisions in the *Standard Oil* and *American Tobacco* cases had for the first time given the antitrust law "an authoritative construction which is workable and intelligible." Taft concluded his address by expressing confidence that the people would ultimately vote for the preservation of the Constitution rather than its destruction.[40]

"I shall not go out to make speeches,"[41] Taft wrote to Nellie in July, attempting to maintain the tradition that overt campaigning was beneath the dignity of a sitting president. But he made an exception for the gramophone, which once again allowed him to speak to voters from the comfort of his summer home in Beverly. On October 1, 1912, Taft recorded excerpts from his acceptance speech called "Popular Unrest," along with six other discs, for the Victor Talking Machine Company. Here is the relevant passage on the Constitution:

After we have changed all the governmental machinery so as to permit instantaneous expression of the people in constitutional amendment, in statute, and in recall of public agent, what then? Votes are not bread, constitutional amendments are not work, referendums do not pay rent or furnish houses, recalls do not furnish clothing, initiatives do not supply employment or relieve inequalities of condition or of opportunity. We still ought to have set before us the definite plans to bring on complete equality of opportunity and to abolish hardship and evil for humanity. We listen for them in vain.[42]

In Taft's other records, he defended his economic achievements and the Constitution. In "On Prosperity," he said that the tariff policy of the Democratic Party would "halt and paralyze business." In a speech on peace, he repeated his call for a world court. In "President Taft on a Protective Tariff," he legalistically insisted that he had fulfilled the promise of the platform of 1908 to revise the tariff at an extra session of Congress. "An extra session was called and the tariff was revised," Taft said defensively. "The platform did not say in specific words that the revision would be generally downward, but I construed it to mean that." He responded to criticism that his vigorous antitrust prosecutions had been bad for business. "The answer to the charge is first, that as long as the statute is upon the statute book, it's the sworn duty of the President and his assistant to see that the law is executed." And in a fervent address called "Who Are the People?" Taft expressed the wan hope that the people would resist Roosevelt's and Wilson's populist siren calls and vote to defend "our popular constitutional representative form of government with the independence of the judiciary as necessary to the preservation of those liberties that are the inheritance of centuries."

On October 14, an assassination attempt against Roosevelt only increased the former president's popular appeal; he bravely declared, "It takes more than that to kill a bull moose" and then finished delivering his ninety-minute speech. Two weeks later, on October 30, Vice President Sherman died of kidney disease; when Taft chose Columbia University president Nicholas Murray Butler to replace him on the ticket, the public reacted with indifference, since everyone anticipated Taft's defeat. "I do not know," Henry Adams exclaimed waspishly, "whether Taft or the *Titanic* is likely to be the furthest reaching disaster."[43] But until the end, Taft vainly hoped for victory and a reconciliation with Roosevelt.[44]

On Election Day, Taft won the fewest electoral votes ever received by an incumbent president, and Roosevelt won the most

electoral votes ever received by a third-party candidate.[45] Taft
carried only two states—Utah and Vermont—receiving 8 electoral votes, while Roosevelt carried six states, with 88 electoral
votes. But in the three-way race, Wilson won an Electoral College landslide, with forty states and 435 electoral votes. In the
end, Wilson won 42 percent of the popular vote; Roosevelt,
27 percent; and Taft, 23 percent, with 6 percent going to the
Socialist candidate, Eugene V. Debs. The Democrats increased
their majority in the House and took the Senate from the Republicans.

In the wake of his decisive defeat, Taft was gracious and
relieved. After wiring his congratulations to Wilson, he wrote
to a friend, "The vote in favor of Mr. Roosevelt was greater
than I expected, and to that extent the result was a disappointment."[46] But Taft was hardly surprised. "In my heart," he wrote,
he was "making preparations for the future to be lived outside
the White House."[47] He told a reporter from the *New York
World* of his gratitude for the presidency and his still lively judicial ambitions. "I am very glad to have had the opportunity to
be President," he confessed. "My tastes had been and still are
judicial, but there is a very wide field of usefulness for a President."[48]

Days after the election, Taft set off for a meeting in New
Haven, Connecticut, where the president of Yale University
offered him the Kent professorship of law on the spot. (As a Yale
official later recalled, Taft joked "that he was afraid that a Chair
would not be adequate, but that if we would provide a Sofa of
Law, it might be all right.")[49] In December, he sent his last written address to the opening of Congress. In a striking expression
of constitutional frustration, he recommended that Congress
require the members of the president's cabinet to attend sessions
of the House and Senate and answer questions about legislation,
as they had done in the early days of the Republic. "This rigid

holding apart of the executive and the legislative branches of this Government has not worked for the great advantage of either,"[50] he confessed. After the new year, Taft sent two final special messages to Congress—the subjects were fur seals, on January 8, and transportation in Alaska, on February 6. In these final weeks of his presidency, Taft's mood began to lighten. "The nearer I get to the inauguration of my successor," he wrote to a friend, "the greater relief I feel."

On February 25, 1913, a week before Wilson took the presidential oath, Taft wrote a letter to the *Yale Daily News*. "I am coming back to Yale," he declared, expressing anxiety that the senior undergraduates might test his "ignorance and forgetfulness" of the law. But "despite these dangers," it gave him "great pleasure" to return because

> there is need that our young men should appreciate the Constitution of the United States, under which we have enjoyed so many blessings and under which we must work out our political and economic salvation. And this need is especially keen in a day when that instrument is regarded so lightly by a class of fanatical enthusiasts seeking short cuts to economic perfection, on the one hand, and by unscrupulous demagogues who to promote their own interests do not hesitate to promote disrespect and even contempt for the Constitution and the laws enacted under it on the other.[51]

The assaults of Wilson and Roosevelt continued to sting.

In the final days of his administration, Taft vetoed two federal laws on constitutional grounds. On February 28, he vetoed the Webb-Kenyon Act, regulating the interstate transport of alcohol, objecting that it unconstitutionally delegated to the states Congress's exclusive power to regulate interstate commerce.

(The Senate overrode his veto the same day, and the House quickly followed.) And on the morning of March 4, 1913, Woodrow Wilson's inauguration day, Taft had one final constitutional duty he was determined to perform. He sent to the House a veto message refusing to approve an appropriations bill on the ground that a provision allocating $300,000 for the enforcement of the antitrust law stipulated that no part of the money should be spent to prosecute any business combination created for the purpose of "increasing of wages, shortening of hours or bettering the condition of labor."[52] Taft called the provision unconstitutional "class legislation of the most vicious sort," as well as a covert attempt to legalize the secondary boycott, which he had questioned as a lower court judge fourteen years earlier. For the judicial president who had never stopped pining for the bench, Taft's last official act had a poetic symmetry.

Later that day, after Wilson was sworn in, Taft and Nellie set out by train to visit Augusta, Georgia, for a well-deserved vacation. Not long after, Taft returned to New Haven to take up his teaching duties at Yale. He was fifty-five years old. The Tafts lived, fittingly enough, in the Hotel Taft, constructed by his brother on the New Haven Green, and then settled into a comfortable house at 367 Prospect Street.[53]

Relieved to be liberated from the stresses of the presidency, Taft returned to his Paleo diet. In a single year, he lost the 75 pounds he had gained during his presidency.[54] On December 12, 1913, he told the *New York Times* that he had weighed exactly 340 pounds on March 4, but now "tipped the scale at exactly 270.8 pounds." "I have lost exactly 69.2 pounds of flesh," he proudly declared.[55] Taft more or less maintained this weight for the rest of his life, and his sleep apnea disappeared. Now alert rather than somnolent in public, he enjoyed a remarkable burst of productivity and wrote a series of important lectures and books without a research assistant,[56] beginning in 1913 with *Popular*

Government: Its Essence, Its Permanence, and Its Perils. He was a popular and conscientious professor at Yale, speaking from notes rather than reading his lectures, and an exam from his constitutional law class included questions such as "What is the power, exactly stated, which the Judicial branch of the Government exercises in respect to acts of Congress?"

Popular Government arose from a series of lectures that defended constitutionalism and representative government and criticized direct democracy.[57] "*Now popular government is not an end*," Taft wrote emphatically. "It is a means of enabling people to live together in communities, municipals, state and national, and under these conditions to secure to each individual and each class of individuals the greatest measure of happiness."[58] The Framers of the Constitution, he noted accurately, did not believe "that the majority could always be trusted certainly to accord to the individual just and equitable treatment in his pursuit of happiness."[59]

Popular Government is an extended explanation for why Taft refused, as president, to court popularity for its own sake. He believed that the president, Congress, and the judiciary should filter public opinion to promote thoughtful deliberation by the people. While Taft sympathized with the progressives' goals of ending corruption, he argued that "the method they propose"— the initiative, referendum, and recall of judges—"and the bitter class spirit they encourage are dangerous in the extreme, and if carried to their logical result will undermine just and enduring popular government."[60]

Recalling the "disastrous results" of the "pure democracies in ancient times," Taft argued that similar proposals now "to dispense with all the limitations upon legislation contained in the Constitution" and to "leave to the initiative and the referendum, without regard to the character of the law, or what it affects, and without limitation as to individual rights, the absolute power to legislate according to the will of the people"[61] would lead to ruin in the United States, as it had in Rome. Taft endorsed James Madison's definition of republicanism, which he described "as a popular representative government,"[62] and he emphasized that law should reflect considered public opinion but not populist whim.

6

"I Love Judges and I Love Courts": Chief Justice at Last

William Howard Taft yearned so ardently to be chief justice that he prepared the groundwork during his own presidency. When Chief Justice Melville Fuller died a year after bungling the administration of Taft's presidential oath, Taft agonized over the appointment of his successor. As the president observed wistfully to Justice William Moody days after Fuller's death in July 1910, "It does seem strange that the one place in the government which I would have liked to fill myself I am forced to give to another."[1]

The obvious candidate was Charles Evans Hughes, the former governor of New York and potential rival to Taft in 1912, whom Taft had shrewdly removed from the political arena by nominating him as an associate justice three months earlier. Just before making that appointment, Taft told his aide Archie Butt, "I don't know the man I admire more than Hughes. If I ever have the chance I shall offer to him the Chief Justiceship."[2] And yet when the opportunity presented itself later that year, Taft could not bring himself to appoint the forty-eight-year-old dynamo, whose youth and perfect health suggested that he would outlive Taft, denying the president any possible opportunity to succeed him. And so in December, after telephoning to cancel a White House interview with Hughes as the justice was dressing for the appointment, Taft instead elevated one of Hughes's colleagues, Justice Edward Douglass White, a Catholic Southern Democrat who, at the reassuringly advanced age of sixty-five, was the oldest chief justice ever nominated. The only explanation for this unusual appointment was the president's hope that White would expire in time for Taft to take his place.

And yet, in the decade that followed, White inconveniently refused to perish. After Warren Harding's election in 1920, Taft visited the president-elect in Marion, Ohio, where Harding astonished and delighted Taft by asking, "Would you accept a position on the Supreme Bench?"[3] Taft replied, with what must have been scarcely concealed emotion, that "it was and always had been the ambition of my life," but since he had twice declined the honor, "I could not accept any place but the chief justiceship."[4] After Harding reassured Taft of his intention to elevate him to the center chair, Taft hastened to Washington to pay a call on Chief Justice White. Appraising the seventy-five-year-old jurist's declining health with a gimlet eye, he was disappointed to discover that White said nothing about retirement. Happily for Taft, the aging chief justice soon fulfilled his hopes by dying without warning on May 19, 1921.

To Taft's frustration, President Harding dithered over the appointment, and so the former president mobilized every lobbying resource at his disposal, dispatching surrogates to emphasize his extensive experience on the federal bench.[5] His postpresidential service, however, proved to be especially compelling: Taft was enjoying a bipartisan surge of popularity owing to his service as co-chairman of the National War Labor Board, which redeemed the "father of injunctions" in the hearts of organized labor because he had supported a series of progressive reforms including collective bargaining, a minimum wage, and bans on "yellow dog" contracts, in which workers agreed not to join unions.[6] At the same time, his work on behalf of international arbitration

and the League of Nations had won over Wilsonian internation-
alists.[7] A final push by Attorney General Harry Daugherty convinced Harding that Taft's administrative skills would help clear
the congestion in the federal courts resulting from the recent
enactment of Prohibition and the many arrests justified in the
name of the war on alcohol.[8] And so, on June 30, 1921, Harding
nominated the man he affectionately called "the Big Chief" to
be the tenth chief justice of the United States. The Senate confirmed the nomination the same day, by an overwhelming vote
of 60 to 4.[9] Taft viewed his appointment not only as the fulfill-
ment of his lifelong dream but also as vindication for his electoral defeat nearly a decade earlier. The praise for his nomination
was evidence, he suggested, that "I have come back from the
status in which the campaign of 1912 left me."[10]

On July 11, Taft was sworn in as chief justice. When Justice
Joseph McKenna repeated the ceremony on October 3, the first
day of the new term, he forgot to bring an official copy of the
oath, and Taft was impressed that his new colleague recited it
from memory.[11] Taft threw himself into the job with passion and
discipline, imposing on himself a schedule that dispelled any of
the accusations of laziness that had followed him during his
unwanted presidency. Freed from the burdens of the sleep apnea
that had been caused by his presidential obesity, he would awaken
at 5:15 a.m., repair to his study (the justices in those days worked
from home), and toil until breakfast at 8. After more work until
10, he walked from his home to the Capitol, where the Court
then sat, usually crossing the bridge that carries Connecticut
Avenue across Rock Creek Park, known today as the Taft Bridge.
After hearing cases at the Court from noon until 4:30, he was
driven home, where he worked from 5 until 10, with an hour for
dinner. "If I can maintain this," he wrote to Horace Taft, "I think
I shall have time enough to do the work. You see it gives me, in
addition to my court work of four hours, eight hours for work
outside the court, two hours for meals, and seven hours for sleep,

one hour for exercise and one hour for dressing. This makes twenty-three hours. Just where the other hour goes you can figure out for yourself—I haven't time."[12]

Out of the 1,596 opinions delivered by the Court during his nine years as chief justice, Taft wrote one-sixth of the total himself, averaging 30 opinions a term while his colleagues averaged 20.[13] And having achieved his dream job, Taft found that it surpassed his expectations of happiness. "Next to my wife and children," the Court "is the nearest thing to my heart in life,"[14] he wrote. "The truth is," he observed in 1925, "I don't remember I ever was president."[15]

Taft began his chief justiceship with an ambitious vision of what he hoped to achieve for the judiciary, a vision he had clearly set out as president. Drawing on his executive experience, he aspired to nothing less than reform of the administrative structure of the entire federal judiciary, making it fully equal in independence, power, and dignity to the White House and Congress. "I love judges, and I love courts," he once enthused. "They are my ideals on earth of what we shall meet afterward in heaven under a just God."[16] And Taft was able to achieve as chief justice the constitutional vision that had eluded him as president, exercising executive leadership that had been absent from the Court since the tenure of the greatest chief justice, John Marshall. The legal scholar Robert Post has written that "it was Taft who, as former chief magistrate of the Executive Branch, transformed the role of Chief Justice into something analogous to a chief executive for the judicial branch of government."[17] Taft was convinced that "the efficient administration of justice" would help the federal judiciary defend the Constitution against populist threats posed by state legislatures and juries and also keep the president and Congress within their constitutionally appointed bounds. And in so doing, he created the modern federal judiciary as a separate and cohesive branch of government.

Days after he joined the Court, Taft plunged into the ambitious task of judicial reform for which he had been preparing his entire life. Taft had campaigned for president in 1908 on the need to improve the efficiency of court administration. *"The greatest question now before the American public* is the improvement of the administration of justice, civil and criminal, both in the matter of its prompt dispatch and the cheapening of its use," he had declared forcefully during the campaign.[18] As president, he had proved his mettle as an extraordinary administrator. The historian Paolo Coletta has observed that Taft was "the first president to have the federal administration studied in detail as one mechanism," and Taft became known as the "efficiency engineer" for reorganizing the Departments of War, State, and Treasury, and the Customs Service, as well as creating the Commission on Economy and Efficiency and attempting to send Congress the first centralized executive budget.[19] Charles Evans Hughes said that efficient administration of justice was "the dominant interest of [Taft's] public life."[20]

As chief justice, Taft controversially lobbied Congress to achieve his visionary program of improving the efficient administration of the federal courts. (He had scorned similar lobbying as president but seems to have believed that his constitutional role had changed.) Taft had three ambitious goals, and he achieved all of them.[21] First, he persuaded Congress in 1922 to establish a judicial conference of federal appellate judges, led by the chief justice. Second, he persuaded Congress to pass the Judiciary Act of 1925, which gave the Court discretion to focus on constitutional cases rather than being forced to hear mandatory appeals of less consequential disputes. And finally, he secured the necessary funds to build a magnificent Supreme Court building across the street from the Capitol, relieving the justices of the indignity of convening in the old Senate chamber in the basement of the Capitol building. Designed by Cass Gilbert, the Temple of Justice is the most tangible monument to Taft's constitutional vision of the Supreme Court as head of a separate and fully equal branch of government, as inspiring as the Capitol and the White House themselves.

The 1922 legislation accomplished nothing less than the unification of the federal judiciary in the same way that Taft had attempted to unify the administration of the executive branch. Taft advocated a "flying squadron" of roving judges who could be assigned to congested courts by the chief justice, in the hope that a more efficient judiciary would be less vulnerable to congressional attempts to restrict its jurisdiction and end life tenure. The act also created the Conference of Senior Circuit Judges, including twenty-four temporary judgeships, providing "the first formal mechanism by which members of the federal judiciary might develop national administrative policies, reassign judges temporarily, and recommend legislation," in the words of the Federal Judicial Center.[22] This expansion in the machinery of the federal judiciary allowed the chief justice, as Taft put it, "temporarily to mass the force of the judiciary where the arrears are greatest."[23] Taft praised the legislation for introducing into a previously disorganized and decentralized judicial system "an executive principle to secure effective teamwork."[24] Taft viewed his role as the head of the newly created judicial conference like that of a president leading his cabinet, and he offered assistance to individual district court judges who were behind on their caseload.[25] District judges responded gratefully to these reforms. As Judge Learned Hand wrote to Taft, "It is a great comfort to know the interest that you take. To be frank, we have never felt it before your incumbency."[26]

As president, Taft had insisted on the need to strengthen the authority of the federal courts by reforming civil and criminal procedure. In December 1909, in his first message to Congress, he declared that "a change in judicial procedure, with a view to reducing its expense to private litigants in civil cases and facilitating the dispatch of business and final decision in both civil and criminal cases, constitutes the greatest need in our American institutions."[27] (Imagine a president today making a similar claim in a State of the Union address.) And in 1926, the Senate Judiciary Committee endorsed Taft's proposed reforms, which united dozens of confusing separate systems of procedural rules into a single, efficient whole. The Federal Rules of Civil Procedure at last became law in 1938, an enduring monument to Taft's vision of strong federal courts that protected both labor and capital fairly and efficiently, clearing their dockets without delay.

In addition to organizing lower federal judges to act as an efficient and coequal branch of government, Taft lobbied Congress to pass his second great reform, the Judiciary Act of 1925, which gave the Supreme Court control over its own docket. This reform represented the most important change in the Court's procedures since the landmark Judiciary Act of 1789. Before it passed, the Supreme Court was required to hear all cases involving federal rights and laws, under a concept called "mandatory jurisdiction." As early as 1908, in a speech called "Delays and Defects in the Enforcement of Law in This Country," Taft had objected that the volume of cases that the Supreme Court was required to review left it unable to execute its "highest function"—namely, constitutional interpretation. The Court's appellate jurisdiction, he concluded, should be limited accordingly.[28] The 1925 reform achieved Taft's goal, giving the Court the discretion to focus on those cases it believed raised important constitutional questions or questions of federal law about which lower appellate courts disagreed. Thanks to this reform, the backlog in the Court's docket disappeared, and the number of cases decided by the justices plummeted from more than five hundred cases a year in 1924 to fewer than two hundred in 1926.[29] The number of appellate cases decided by full opinion declined by more than half, averaging 30 percent in 1916 and falling to 16 percent in 1928.[30] (Today, the Court writes opinions in about 1 percent of the cases on its docket, agreeing to decide fewer than eighty cases a year.)[31] "The real work [of] the Supreme Court," Taft declared, "is to lay down important principles of law and thus to help the public at large to a knowledge of their rights and duties and to make the law clearer."[32]

Within the increasingly efficient Court, Taft proved himself to be the surest builder of consensus since John Marshall. Deploying his amiable personality and preference for consensus over confrontation to "mass the court," as he put it, Taft, like Marshall, encouraged unanimous opinions and discouraged dissent. He maintained that the Court should preserve its institutional legitimacy by speaking as often as possible in one voice. Two of the six justices whom Taft had appointed while president, Willis Van Devanter and Mahlon Pitney, served with him and welcomed his leadership, although they did not always fulfill his hopes. Even Louis Brandeis, whose nomination to the Court Taft had vigorously opposed in 1916, and who had coolly appraised Taft as a "first-rate second-rate mind,"[33] praised Taft's talent for building consensus and "considerable executive ability."[34] "We are very happy with the present Chief," Oliver Wendell Holmes Jr. concurred. "He is good-humored, laughs readily, not quite rapidly enough, but keeps things moving pleasantly." Holmes added that "never before . . . have we gotten along with so little jangling and dissension."[35]

Taft idolized John Marshall, whom he called "the greatest Judge that America or the World has produced."[36] Once, as he walked past a statue of Marshall on the west side of the Capitol, a companion asked if he would have rather been Marshall than president. "I would rather have been Marshall than any other American unless it had been Washington," Taft replied, "and I am inclined to think I would rather have been Marshall than Washington. He made this country." Continuing on the walk, Taft then stopped and added, "Taking it all in all, I think Washington was the greatest American, the greatest man, I almost believe, of his generation. Marshall is certainly the greatest jurist America has ever produced and Hamilton our greatest constructive statesman."[37]

The chief justice, like the associate justices, has a single vote on the Supreme Court. His only formal power is the authority to assign the writing of an opinion when he is in the majority, to himself or to another justice. Like Marshall, Taft encouraged unanimity by joining majority opinions with which he did not fully agree and encouraging his colleagues to be similarly accommodating.[38] As a result, the Taft Court was remarkably cohesive: 84 percent of its opinions between 1921 and 1928 were unanimous,[39] and only 7 percent were issued with a written dissent.[40] (By way of comparison, about 30 percent of the Court's decisions between 1946 and 2009 were unanimous, a rate that continues today.)[41] As time went on, Taft promoted unanimity by revising his majority opinions to induce skeptical justices to join them. He participated in more than fifteen hundred decisions but dissented in only nineteen—writing or joining the Court's majority opinion in 98.7 percent of cases.[42]

"I don't approve of dissents generally," Taft explained, "for I think in many cases where I differ from the majority, it is more important to stand by the Court and give its judgment weight than merely to record my individual dissent where it is better to have the law certain than to have it settled either way."[43] During his tenure, Taft suppressed more than two hundred of his own dissents,[44] which he deprecated as "a form of egotism" that "only weaken the prestige of the Court."[45] Taft persuaded other justices to do the same.[46] Reflecting this norm, one justice wrote to another, "I do not agree but shall submit."[47]

During the second half of Taft's tenure, however, the unanimity rate on the Court declined, falling to 70 percent in 1929. The reasons for this development included Taft's declining health and the less urgent impulse for the Court to show a united face to defend itself against congressional attacks, which had lessened as time went on.[48] But the most important reason for the decline of unanimity, in an irony that Taft may not have grasped, was Taft's own great achievement: the passage of the Judiciary Act of 1925, which gave the Court the discretion to focus on a handful of hotly contested cases rather than a hodgepodge of uncontroversial ones.[49]

Finally, the most tangible symbol of Taft's belief in the need for the judiciary to be independent from the president and Congress was his determination to create a majestic building for the Court, separate from the Capitol. Since 1860, the Court had met in the chamber vacated when the U.S. Senate moved to its new wing. But the old Senate chamber, although grand in its way, was inadequate for the Court's theatrical purposes—the justices had no backstage dressing area, for example, and had to put on their robes in full view of the gawking spectators. Soon after he became chief justice, Taft learned of legislation pending in Congress that would provide funds for the construction of new federal buildings, and in 1926 he convinced Congress to appropriate funds for the purchase of a new site for the Court, on First Street, across from the Capitol. In 1928, Taft told the House Judiciary Committee that the justices supported the new building by a 5–4 vote. Congress authorized $9,740,000 for construction on December 20, 1929, and Taft chose the architect Cass Gilbert to design it. The result was a marble palace that succeeded in combining "all the beauty, charm and dignity of the Lincoln Memorial," as Gilbert wrote to Taft, with "the practical qualities of a first rate office building."[50] For Taft, who had also served as head of the Lincoln Memorial Commission during his presidency, Gilbert's Roman temple was the architectural embodiment of his vision of the federal judiciary as fully equal in stature and dignity to the legislative and executive branches.[51]

As for judicial philosophy, Taft's constitutional vision on the Court was similar to the one he displayed in the White House. Like Marshall and Hamilton, he was generally a nationalist who broadly construed the powers of Congress and the president, as long as they were clearly defined in the text of the Constitution. At the same time, in the old Federalist spirit, Taft also viewed the Court as the last bulwark in the defense of the constitutional rights of liberty and property against threats posed by state legislatures and juries, whom Taft viewed as especially susceptible to the passions of the mob. For this reason, Taft generally deferred to the prerogatives of Congress and the president while striking down laws that he considered a threat to liberty and property in the states. Ever since his days ruling on labor disputes on the Sixth Circuit, Taft had feared the mob. And on the Supreme Court, Taft was most likely to strike down laws when he thought that mobs in control of state governments were threatening the rights of property and liberty protected by the Fourteenth Amendment. Overall, the Taft Court struck down 131 state laws, while its predecessor the White Court had struck down only 107. By contrast, the Hughes Court, which came after Taft and was less devoted to freedom of contract, struck down 78 state laws.[52]

Taft's first major opinion, handed down on December 21, 1921, allowed him to write into law the protections for the use of injunctions in labor disputes that had led his critics to denounce him as the "father of injunctions." In *Truax v. Corrigan*, Taft wrote an opinion for a 5–4 majority striking down an Arizona law that forbade state courts from issuing injunctions in labor disputes, except when "necessary to prevent irreparable injury to property or to a property right." Taft used the case to inscribe by judicial fiat the distinction between legal and illegal boycotts that, as president, he had unsuccessfully tried to persuade Congress to enact.[53] Taft's willingness to circumvent Congress as a judge but not as president shows that, although he generally deferred to the executive and legislative branches when they operated within broad but constrained constitutional limits, he was committed to enforcing his vision of the

Constitution rather than an unwavering advocate of judicial restraint.

But when Congress rather than the states passed economic regulations, Taft generally voted to uphold them. (The Taft Court as a whole struck down only twelve federal laws—the same number as the White Court—while the Hughes Court struck down fourteen.)[54] And Taft, unlike some of his conservative colleagues, was not a Jeffersonian libertarian, consistently ruling for liberty of contract regardless of the source of the regulation. Instead, he was, above all, a Hamiltonian nationalist, who broadly construed Congress's power to regulate the economy as well as to protect public safety. On May 1, 1922, he wrote the majority opinion for the Court in *Stafford v. Wallace*, recognizing Congress's broad authority under the Commerce Clause to pass the Packers and Stockyards Act of 1921, which regulated the shipping of meat and livestock through interstate commerce.

And yet two weeks later, Taft held that Congress's regulatory efforts had gone too far. On May 15, 1922, he wrote the opinion for a unanimous Court in *Bailey v. Drexel Furniture Co.*,[55] striking down the federal Child Labor Tax Law, which imposed a tax on businesses employing children under the age of fourteen. Taft was so successful in massing the Court that he persuaded the champions of judicial restraint, Brandeis and Holmes, to suppress what must have been their jurisprudential disagreement.[56] Taft concluded that the federal child labor tax was not a permissible attempt to raise tax revenue but an impermissible attempt to intrude on the state's authority to regulate the hours of labor.[57] Taft worried that upholding the law as a tax would remove all limits on Congress's power to regulate interstate commerce.[58] (In 2012, Justice Antonin Scalia voiced the same concerns and cited Taft's opinion at length in his dissent from the Court's 5–4 decision to uphold the Affordable Care Act as a tax.)

The child labor case, however, was an exception to Taft's general determination to defer to Congress. In 1923, he filed a significant dissent (the act of dissenting itself must have pained his Marshallian spirit) in *Adkins v. Children's Hospital*,[59] in which the Court struck down a federal minimum wage law for women. Writing for a 5–3 majority, Justice George Sutherland held that freedom of contract could be abridged only in "exceptional circumstances." Taft, like Marshall, was devoted to freedom of contract, but as co-chairman of the National War Labor Board during the Great War, he had wondered aloud about how munitions and textile workers could live on their low wages. Taft's dissent in *Adkins* may have been informed by that experience, since it includes some of his most memorable language about the excesses of unregulated capitalism. The poorest employees, he wrote, "are peculiarly subject to the overreaching of the harsh and greedy employer. The evils of the sweating system and of the long hours and low wages which are characteristic of it are well known."[60] Taft's dissent was vindicated in 1937 when his successor as chief justice, Charles Evans Hughes, wrote for a 5–4 majority of the Court overturning the *Adkins* decision and upholding a Washington State law that required a minimum wage for women.

Much of the Taft Court's caseload involved a backlog of criminal cases arising from Prohibition. Before joining the Court, Taft had opposed Prohibition on the ground that it would represent a dangerous expansion in the powers of Congress, threatening local self-government and states' rights, and transferring the business of manufacturing alcohol to the criminal classes.[61] As chief justice, however, Taft set aside his personal opposition to Prohibition and faithfully voted to uphold convictions under the Volstead Act, the draconian federal law passed to enforce the Eighteenth Amendment. (Taft's insistence on maintaining a dry home during Prohibition out of respect for the Constitution provoked the only major disagreement between Taft and Nellie in their long marriage; eventually, Taft, never a heavy drinker, refused to discuss the issue with his wife.)[62] For Taft, citizens and judges had an obligation to respect all provisions of the Constitution, regardless of their personal views.[63]

Taft's most famous opinions are those upholding criminal convictions in the war against alcohol. In *Carroll v. United States* (1925),[64] Taft created the "automobile exception" to the Fourth Amendment to the Constitution. In passing the Volstead Act, Congress distinguished between searches of private residences, where warrants were required, and searches of cars, where they were not. Writing for a 7–2 majority, Taft upheld the law against a Fourth Amendment challenge, noting that ever since the Founding, courts had distinguished between homes and movable objects. Similarly, in *Olmstead v. United States* (1928), Taft wrote for a 5–4 majority upholding the warrantless wiretapping of one of America's most successful bootleggers. In his opinion, a straightforward if wooden application of the original understanding of the Constitution, Taft held that the government had not violated the Fourth Amendment when it placed a wiretap on phone lines leading into the bootlegger's office because the Framers defined "unreasonable searches and seizures" as those involving physical trespass against private property. (Here, the wiretaps had been placed under public sidewalks.) Brandeis's visionary dissenting opinion, the greatest defense of electronic privacy in the twentieth century, was vindicated when the Supreme Court overturned Taft's opinion in the *Katz* case in 1967.

In the Hamiltonian spirit, Taft broadly construed presidential power as well as congressional power. On October 25, 1926, Taft delivered the most significant opinion of his entire tenure, *Myers v. United States*,[65] in which he held that the president alone has the power to fire officers he appoints. Taft would later say of his opinion in *Myers*, "I never wrote an opinion that I felt to be so important in its effect."[66] The case involved the president's power to fire executive branch officials without being constrained by Congress, and it remains a milestone for those who take a broad view of executive power today. In 1876, in the wake of the

impeachment of President Andrew Johnson, Congress passed a
law declaring that postmasters could be appointed and removed
by the president only with the consent of the Senate. In 1920,
President Woodrow Wilson had fired a postmaster named Myers
without the Senate's consent, and Myers insisted that his firing
violated the 1876 law. In a seventy-one-page opinion for the
Court, Taft reviewed the text and the original understanding of
the Constitution, as well as subsequent interpretations of the
scope of presidential power by courts, congresses, and presidents.
Under Article II of the Constitution, Taft concluded, the president has the exclusive power to fire any executive officer whom
he had appointed with the advice and consent of the Senate, and
any attempt by Congress to restrict this power is unconstitutional. He seemed to draw on his own experience as president in
insisting that the chief magistrate needed an unlimited power to
fire executive officials in order to take care that the laws are faithfully executed. "The natural meaning of the term 'executive
power' granted the President included the appointment and
removal of executive subordinates,"[67] Taft wrote.

> In all such cases, the discretion to be exercised is that of
> the President in determining the national public interest
> and in directing the action to be taken by his executive sub-
> ordinates to protect it. . . . The moment that he loses con-
> fidence in the intelligence, ability, judgment or loyalty of
> anyone of them, he must have the power to remove him
> without delay. To require him to file charges and submit
> them to the consideration of the Senate might make impos-
> sible that unity and coordination in executive administra-
> tion essential to effective action.[68]

In a powerful dissent, Brandeis insisted that Taft had conflated
"high political offices," such as cabinet secretaries, whom the president should have sole discretion to fire, and "inferior offices," such

as postmasters, whose removal Congress should be able to restrict. "The doctrine of the separation of powers was adopted by the convention of 1787 not to promote efficiency, but to preclude the exercise of arbitrary power," Brandeis memorably declared.[69] Brandeis's history, as well as his prose, was arguably more persuasive than Taft's—and the Supreme Court recognized as much in a later case, *Humphrey's Executor v. United States* (1935),[70] in which it unanimously held that Congress could restrict the president from firing an officer on the Federal Trade Commission because Congress had the power to create "quasi-legislative or quasi-judicial agencies" and "to require them to act in discharge of their duties independently of executive control."[71] Nevertheless, Taft's opinion has been praised as a "masterpiece of judicial craftsmanship" by judges and scholars today who believe that the Constitution gives the president broad, "unitary" executive power to supervise foreign affairs and the executive branch without being constrained by Congress.[72]

"Chief Justice Taft was the mirror image of Professor Taft!" the historian Francis Graham Lee has observed. "Taft's opinion in *Myers* seemed totally to contradict the view he earlier expressed in *Our Chief Magistrate and His Powers*."[73] In fact, however, there is no contradiction. "Once power was delegated to the Chief Executive," observe three leading proponents of the "unitary executive theory," Taft believed that "the president should be given broad and plenary control over those powers."[74] After all, they note, Taft fired Gifford Pinchot in part because of his belief in the importance of unifying presidential control over the executive branch. In other words, Taft believed that the president's power, like that of Congress, was broad but constrained within the boundaries explicitly set out in the Constitution.

In the second half of the 1920s, Taft became close to the conservative justices George Sutherland and Pierce Butler, and his votes to invalidate progressive legislation in the name of property rights helped contribute to the Court's subsequent attempts to strike down Franklin Roosevelt's New Deal. Nevertheless, Taft's administrative reforms shoring up judicial independence prepared the ground for the vigorous enforcement of the Bill of Rights and the post–Civil War amendments that has defined the Court in the decades since it struck down school segregation in *Brown v. Board of Education* in 1954. Taft's policies as president were less racist than Woodrow Wilson, who expanded segregation in the federal government, or even Theodore Roosevelt, who dishonorably discharged African American troops. In the tradition of his father, who was devoted to equal civil rights for all, Taft insisted in his inaugural address that he did not have "the slightest race prejudice or feeling," and he pledged "sympathy for those who bear it or suffer from it."[75] At the same time, Taft refused to support the hiring of Republican African American officeholders in the South, in a futile effort to entice Southern Democrats to join the Republican Party. And although he spoke extensively as president on the need to expand education for African Americans, Taft wrote a unanimous opinion for the Supreme Court in 1927 upholding a Mississippi law requiring a Chinese American citizen to attend a local segregated school, open only to "colored children of the brown, yellow, or black races." Citing the precedent of *Plessy v. Ferguson*, which upheld the constitutionality of racially segregated railroad cars, Taft concluded, "The decision is within the discretion of the state in regulating its public schools, and does not conflict with the Fourteenth Amendment."[76] In other words, although Taft was a public champion of civil rights for all races, he joined his eight fellow justices in applying what appeared at the time to be clear judicial precedent.

As the 1920s drew to a close, Taft's health declined. Although his weight remained under control—he weighed about 280 pounds during his final years, far less than his presidential weight of 340 pounds—he had suffered heart attacks in 1924 and 1926, and his blood pressure had risen due to arteriosclerosis.[77] "I am really in an invalid state," Taft wrote in 1928.[78] Taft's memory began to slip, and he stumbled slightly in administering the oath of office to President Herbert Hoover in March 1929, as the ceremony was broadcast for the first time by radio.[79] (After a young girl from New York wrote to correct his mistake, Taft replied that she could "attribute the variation" in the words of the oath "to the defect of an old man's memory.")[80] In January 1930, while visiting Cincinnati for his brother Charles's funeral, Taft suffered hallucinations, and he set off with Nellie for rest in North Carolina. But he recognized that his powers were waning, and so, on February 3, the ailing chief justice wrote a letter to President Hoover resigning from the Court. "Lifted off the train at the Union Station" in Washington, Pringle writes, "he was wheeled to an automobile and all that came from his lips was an occasional 'darling' when Mrs. Taft was near."[81] He was put to bed in his house on Wyoming Avenue and never arose. On his deathbed, Taft read a tender letter by Justice Holmes and signed by all of the members of the Court.

> We call you Chief Justice still—for we cannot give up the title by which we have known you all these later years and which you have made dear to us. We cannot let you leave us without trying to tell you how dear you have made it. You came to us from achievement in other fields and with the prestige of the illustrious place that you lately had held and you showed us in new form your voluminous capacity for getting work done, your humor that smoothed the tough places, your golden heart that brought you love from every side and most of all from your brethren whose tasks you have made happy and light. We grieve at your illness, but your spirit has given life an impulse that will abide whether you are with us or away.[82]

A month after his resignation, on the evening of Saturday, March 8, 1930, William Howard Taft died. He was seventy-two years old. In the rotunda of the Capitol, as his body lay in state, Gilbert's model of the Supreme Court building was exhibited at his side. In October 1932, at the groundbreaking ceremony for the Temple of Justice, a photograph of Taft was placed in the cornerstone.[83] (Today, Taft's portrait hangs in the West Conference Room and his bust in the center hall.) During the ceremony, Chief Justice Charles Evans Hughes, who had finally achieved the center chair, paid a graceful tribute to his predecessor. "We are indebted to the late Chief Justice William Howard Taft more than anyone else," he declared. "The building is the result of his intelligent persistence."[84]

Epilogue

Our Constitutional President

In April 1922, at his summer home on Cape Cod, Louis Brandeis asked his friend the Harvard law professor Felix Frankfurter, "Felix, do you still think Taft was as bad a president as we thought he was?" Brandeis then added, "It's difficult for me to understand why a man who is so good as Chief Justice, in his function as presiding officer, could have been so bad as President. How do you explain that?" Frankfurter's response: "The explanation is simple. He loathed being President and being Chief Justice [is] all happiness for him."[1]

Frankfurter's explanation was accurate but incomplete. It is true that Taft chafed as a judicial president and thrived as a presidential chief justice because he worshipped the Constitution, had a judicial temperament, and deployed his presidential talent for administration to reform the judicial branch. And yet, viewing Taft's record as president and chief justice in isolation fails to acknowledge the magnitude of his constitutional achievements.

A balanced assessment of Taft's presidency comes from the political scientist Peri Arnold.

Historical judgment makes Taft a mediocrity. But that assessment assumes a new criterion for success. Taft failed to meet expectations for his presidency stimulated by Roosevelt's performance in office as well as the period's mood of political reform. However . . . he was not simply a throwback to an earlier constrained presidency. A wave of important progressive legislation continued during his term in office. But Taft failed very publicly to comprehend the presidency's new responsibilities for popular leadership.[2]

If Taft is judged on his own terms, and not by the twentieth-century standards for a popular presidency set by Roosevelt and Wilson, Arnold concludes, his presidency must be judged more charitably.

Removed from the passions of the Progressive Era political struggles, and not sandwiched between Roosevelt and Wilson, Taft's presidency would be seen as successful. Compared to the norms of the party period presidency, Taft's initiatives were notably aggressive. He passed more reform legislation in his four years than Roosevelt had in his seven years.[3]

Of course, Taft's success as a reformer built on what Roosevelt began and reflected Taft's skills as an administrator rather than an inspiring popular leader. Taft's distinctive contribution was to work with Congress to create the "machinery of government," as he put it, that allowed checks on the excesses of monopoly power—from environmental protection to antitrust enforcement—without interfering with the free market. As Taft wrote to Nellie at the end of his term, "I have strengthened the Supreme Bench, have given them a good deal of new and valuable legislation, have not interfered with business, have kept the peace, and on the whole have led people to pursue their various occupations without interruption. It is a very humdrum, uninteresting administration, and does not attract the attention or enthusiasm of anybody, but after I am out I think that you and I can look back to some pleasure in having done something for the benefit of the public weal."[4]

In calling his administration "humdrum" and "uninteresting," Taft was being too modest. At his best, Taft shows what a constitutional, rather than a popular, conception of the office of the presidency can achieve. It was his refusal to compromise his principles for the sake of reelection that led Taft to denounce the northwestern farmers who threatened to oppose him unless he withdrew his support of Canadian free trade, or to buck the demands of his own party that he start a war with Mexico. And his refusal to circumvent Congress's legislative authority by executive orders, in areas from foreign policy to the tariff, led to moderate policies with broad bipartisan support that were sustained by the next administration, even after the Democrats won the presidency and control of Congress. The Wilson administration completed the downward tariff revision that the Taft administration began, and Wilson's League of Nations built on Taft's vision of an international arbitration system ruled by law rather than force.

Most significantly, Taft's respect for the constitutional powers and limitations of the presidency, Congress, and the judiciary helped him promote the thoughtful deliberation that Madison and Hamilton considered necessary for the success of the American republic. Taft himself contrasted his judicial perspective to that of Roosevelt, perceptively comparing Roosevelt to the populist Andrew Jackson. "There is a decided similarity between Andrew Jackson and Roosevelt," Taft told Archie Butt. "He had the same disrespect for law when he felt the law stood between him and what he thought was right to do."[5] By contrast, Taft's overriding goal as president and as chief justice was to exercise the powers of each office as vigorously as possible within constitutional bounds while resisting populist pressures that threatened the rule of law. In this noble goal, he impressively succeeded. Butt gives a striking example of Taft's readiness to send federal troops in June 1909 to subdue racist white strikers who were attempting to displace African American firemen on the Georgia Railroad. Taft expressed astonishment at a public official who had expressed sympathy with the strikers. "If the leaders of the people are going to pander to this prejudice," Taft asked, "what can we hope from the lower classes?" (Taft was acting here as less a champion of civil rights than as a foe of organized labor.) As Butt concluded, "President Taft will do anything if he has the law on which to base his act. The law to President Taft is the same support as some zealots get from great religious faith. And the fact that the law is unpopular would not cause him to hesitate a minute."[6]

The question of whether the United States should be more of a direct democracy or a representative republic, with broad but limited executive power checked by an independent Congress and judiciary, each with broad but limited powers of their own, dates back to the Constitutional Convention itself. The Founding era's debates between the constitutionalist James Madison and the populist James Wilson recurred throughout the nineteenth century, during the Jacksonian, Civil War, and Reconstruction eras. Taft's presidency, therefore, marked an important phase in what has been a recurring and central tension in American history. Although Presidents Calvin Coolidge and Herbert Hoover adhered to Taft's strict constructionist vision of the presidency, all presidents since Franklin D. Roosevelt have embraced what the historian Arthur M. Schlesinger Jr. called the imperial presidency, drawing on Theodore Roosevelt's and Woodrow Wilson's idea of the president as a steward of the people.

Taft's vigorous but constrained view of the presidency, however, should not be considered a constitutional anachronism. In *Our Chief Magistrate and His Powers*, published in 1916, Taft made clear that he saw the president's powers—from executive privilege to control over the executive branch—as so broad that they were virtually unlimited, as long as they could be linked to specific provisions of the Constitution. Taft's conception of the presidency as a constitutional rather than a popular office—expansive in content, limited in form, and both empowered and constrained by the Constitution[7]—reflected his Madisonian view that the Framers had created a representative republic rather than a direct democracy, headed by a president who would encourage "the sobering effect of deliberation and discussion" by the people over time rather than reflecting the passions of the moment.[8] He maintained this view in the White House, vetoing the admission of New Mexico and Arizona into the Union as states because their constitutions provided for the recall of judicial decisions, and he defended this view extensively after his presidency. In *Liberty Under Law*, Taft anticipated the dangers of making fundamental constitutional changes by a single popular referendum, like Brexit in our own time.

> A popular constituency may be misled by vigorous misrepresentation and denunciation. The shorter the time the people have to think, the better for the demagogue. One of the great difficulties in carrying on popular government is in getting into the heads of the intelligent voters what the real facts are and what reasonable deductions should be made from them. Any reasonable suspension of popular action until calm public consideration of reliable evidence can be secured is in the interest of a wise decision. That at least was what our forefathers thought in making our Federal Government and the result has vindicated them.[9]

Taft's judicial conception of public office made him an effective leader in institutions such as the civil governorship of the

Philippines or on the Supreme Court, where his authority did not depend on popular approval, and he could preside over thoughtful deliberation among a small, elite group. At the same time, Taft showed the limitations as well as the strengths of trying to translate the Founders' eighteenth-century conception of the presidency into the twentieth century. Taft's refusal to "play a part for popularity," as he told Archie Butt, led Butt to lament the public's failure to appreciate him. "In many ways he is the best man I have ever known, too honest for the Presidency, possibly, and possibly too good-natured or too trusting or too something on which it is hard just now for a contemporary to put his finger, but on which the finger of the historian of our politics will be placed with accuracy," Butt wrote. "What really makes me almost ill with indignation, at times, is the fact that we have all our lives heard the American people say: 'Oh, if we only had a President who could act with independence and not be hampered by the second-term fetish.' And here they have one and they don't even appreciate the fact; if they do, it gives only cause for criticism."[10]

Taft purported to be untroubled by the public's indifference. "There are other and better things than being exceedingly popular," Taft told Butt. "Roosevelt was exceedingly popular, and still is in many quarters for reasons that I should not like to have attributed to me." But Taft's refusal to "play a part for popularity" led to a series of political blunders that ultimately alienated Roosevelt and split the Republican Party. And because Taft had no political capital, he couldn't achieve some of the reforms he sought, leading to Republican congressional losses in 1910 and the disintegration of the party in the presidential election of 1912.

Taft's refusal to engage in the art of politics was a product of his constitutional conception of the presidency. "The training of a Judge is something that leads you to depend upon the opinion published and the decree entered as speaking for themselves," he acknowledged.[11] But his political woes also stemmed from a thin-skinned sensitivity to criticism that sometimes clashed with his otherwise judicial temperament. "I have never known a man to dislike discord as much as the President. He wants every man's approval, and a row of any kind is repugnant to him," Archie Butt recalled.[12] As a result, as the historian Doris Kearns Goodwin has described, he failed to court the newly empowered populist press. As Butt recorded in the summer of 1910, "He told the newspaper men the other day that he would not stand the repeated hammerings they were giving him, that he did not have to, and that sooner than stand them he would throw up the job. The worst mistake he ever made was to let them think they could get under his skin, for they are remorseless when they find out they can wound."[13]

Taft's prickly demands for personal loyalty also served to undermine his political effectiveness. "If a public man can deduce any facts he will listen and act accordingly, but he is not swayed in the least against one merely because someone else is prejudiced," Butt observed. "But when he takes a dislike to anyone it is for some reason known to himself, and he does not easily forgive. He is persistent in his antipathies. Mr. Roosevelt once said that Mr. Taft was one of the best haters he had ever known, and I have found this to be true."[14] Taft's instinct to lash out against those he considered disloyal led him to fire aides—including Louis Glavis and Gifford Pinchot—heedless of the political cost. "Whether his indifference to people in general comes from his experience on the bench or whether it comes from a high sense of what he owes to the state, or is in line with his sense of duty, I do not know," Butt observed, "but I do know that he can remove people from office, that he can refuse to grant favors, with an indifference which is impossible to most men of his apparent type."[15]

Taft's judicial presidency was less successful than his presidential chief justiceship because, in attempting to govern the United States in the early twentieth century along the lines that the

Framers clearly preferred, Taft was unable to grapple with forces that the Framers would have abhorred—including the democratization of politics and the increasing power of political parties. By creating an executive with energy, to use Hamilton's term, the Framers left the office open to alterations that ran against their basic conceptions of how the entire federal government should operate.

Today, however, as new populist forces in America and around the world threaten principles of constitutionalism, limited government, democratic deliberation, checks and balances, and the rule of law, Taft's conception of a vigorous but constrained presidency checked by similarly vigorous but constrained courts and Congress looks increasingly appealing. Taft would have been distressed by the spectacle of tweeting presidents and representatives: like Madison in Federalist 10, he believed that direct communication between representatives and their constituents was the democratic vice most to be avoided, since it promoted faction and discouraged reasoned deliberation. Taft predicted the congressional polarization and rule by minority factions that would result when the great parties lost their authority to be moderating forces of unity and compromise. His preference for extended deliberations by the people's representatives rather than impulsive judgments by factions of the people themselves looks prescient as the growing transparency of the White House and Congress, fueled by the 24/7 news cycle, has made bipartisan compromise increasingly elusive. His Madisonian insistence on slow and thoughtful deliberation over time seems both imperative and elusive in an age of instant polling, Twitter mobs, and Facebook likes as substitutes for engaged political debate. His conviction that the republic would falter unless voters took the time calmly to educate themselves about what he called "real facts" and "reliable evidence" before making up their minds seems especially salient in an age of filter bubbles and fake news. Finally, there is the federal judiciary, whose cohesive strength as an arm of government is largely a tribute to Taft's administrative and constitutional vision. As independent judges represent the last check on unconstitutional encroachments by the president, Congress, and the states, conservatives, classical liberals, and progressives alike are converging around a renewed appreciation for judicial independence. And Taft's Madisonian appeals to the people to educate themselves to exercise "voluntary self-restraint" in order to resist demagogues and to promote public deliberation now seems not archaic but prophetic.

These are anxious times, in America and around the world, in which constitutional limitations on executive power, and the independent judges necessary to enforce them, are under attack from populist politicians, amplified by social media technologies that channel and intensify divisive passions. William Howard Taft devoted his career, as president and chief justice, to defending the constitutional structures that divided the powers of the executive, legislative, and judicial branches, filtered the will of the people, and encouraged thoughtful deliberation among their representatives. The populist forces that Taft assailed as our most judicial president and presidential chief justice once again threaten to undermine the Constitution in precisely the ways that Taft predicted. The fact that all three branches today are institutionally equipped, if they choose, to resist these populist threats and to defend the rule of law is an inspiring tribute to Taft's constitutional legacy.

Notes

INTRODUCTION

1. Helen Herron Taft, *Recollections of Full Years* (New York: Dodd, Mead, 1914), 61, https://archive.org/details/recollectionsfu02taft goog.
2. Ibid., 61–62.
3. "Presidential Historians Survey 2017," C-SPAN, https://www.c -span.org/presidentsurvey2017/?page=overall [https://perma.cc /YUV8-LFVL].
4. Roy M. Mersky and Albert P. Blaustein, Survey (1993), reprinted in William G. Ross, "The Ratings Game: Factors That Influence Judicial Reputation," *Marquette Law Review* 79 (1996): app. I.
5. William Howard Taft, *Popular Government: Its Essence, Its Permanence, and Its Perils*, in *The Collected Works of William Howard Taft*, vol. 5, ed. David Potash and Donald F. Anderson (Athens: Ohio University Press, 2003), 100.
6. Henry F. Pringle, *The Life and Times of William Howard Taft*, vol. 1 (Norwalk, CT: Easton Press, 1986), 100.
7. Alpheus Thomas Mason, *William Howard Taft: Chief Justice* (New York: Simon & Schuster, 1965), 13.
8. Jonathan Lurie, *William Howard Taft: The Travails of a Progressive Conservative* (New York: Cambridge University Press, 2012), xii.
9. Lawrence F. Abbott, ed., *Taft and Roosevelt: The Intimate Letters of Archie Butt, Military Aide*, vol. 1 (Garden City, NY: Doubleday, Doran, 1930), 298.
10. William Howard Taft, "Speech Accepting the Nomination for the Presidency by the Republican National Committee," Aug. 1, 1912,

in *The Republican Campaign Text-Book*, Republican National Committee (1912): 11, https://hdl.handle.net/2027/hvd.hw2hd8.

11. Alpheus Thomas Mason, "President By Chance, Chief Justice By Choice," *American Bar Association Journal* 55 (1969): 39.

12. William Howard Taft, "Address at Georgia State Fair Grounds on Wisdom and Necessity of Following the Law," Nov. 4, 1909, in *The Collected Works of William Howard Taft*, vol. 3, ed. David H. Burton (Athens: Ohio University Press, 2002), 323.

13. Theodore Roosevelt, "The Presidency; Making an Old Party Progressive," in *An Autobiography (1858–1919)* (New York: Macmillan, 1913; Bartleby.com, 1998), http://www.bartleby.com/55/10 .html [https://perma.cc/J5DT-CVJP].

14. William Howard Taft, *The President and His Powers*, in *The Collected Works of William Howard Taft*, vol. 6, ed. W. Carey McWilliams and Frank X. Gerrity (Athens: Ohio University Press, 2003), 104. (Originally published in 1916 as *Our Chief Magistrate and His Powers*.)

15. George Will, "Speech at the National Constitution Center's Madisonian Commission Launch," Apr. 13, 2017, C-SPAN, https:// www.c-span.org/video/?426869-1/national-constitution-center -marks-freedom-day.

16. William Howard Taft, *Liberty Under Law: An Interpretation of the Principles of Our Constitutional Government*, in *The Collected Works of William Howard Taft*, vol. 8, ed. Francis Graham Lee (Athens: Ohio University Press, 2004), 5.

17. Ibid., 5–7.

18. Doris Kearns Goodwin, *The Bully Pulpit: Theodore Roosevelt, William Howard Taft, and the Golden Age of Journalism* (New York: Simon & Schuster Paperbacks, 2013), 26.

19. Mason, *Taft: Chief Justice*, 39.

20. Phil Edwards, "The Truth about William Howard Taft's Bathtub," *TriviaHappy*, June 25, 2014, https://triviahappy.com/articles/the -truth-about-william-howard-tafts-bathtub [https://perma.cc /RK72-BRQY]; Alexis Coe, "William Howard Taft Is Still Stuck in the Tub," *New York Times*, Sept. 15, 2017.

21. Scott Bomboy, "Clearing up the William Howard Taft Bathtub Myth," *Constitution Daily*, Feb. 6, 2013, http://blog.constitutioncenter .org/2013/02/why-william-howard-taft-was-probably-never-stuck -in-his-bathtub/ [https://perma.cc/8BL2-S6HU].

22. Edwards, "Taft's Bathtub."

23. "Friends Amused by Taft Bath Story," *Enterprise*, Nov. 3, 1909, in "Chronicling America: Historic American Newspapers," Library of Congress, http://chroniclingamerica.loc.gov/lccn/sn83025323 /1909-11-03/ed-1/seq-7/.// [https://perma.cc/3GPA-9EAE].

24. "Taft Causes Hotel Deluge," *New York Times*, June 19, 1915, 6.
25. Dan Steinberg, "Nats Will Name William Howard Taft New Racing President," *Washington Post*, Jan. 25, 2013, https://www .washingtonpost.com/news/dc-sports-bog/wp/2013/01/25/nats -will-name-william-howard-taft-new-racing-president/?utm _term=.4f94251ef41e [https://perma.cc/R65U-ST8L].
26. Pringle, *Taft*, vol. 1, 20.
27. Henry F. Pringle, *The Life and Times of William Howard Taft*, vol. 2 (Norwalk, CT: Easton Press, 1986), 1072.
28. Andrew Dolan, *The Taft Diet: How President Taft Lost 76 Pounds* (CreateSpace Independent Publishing Platform, 2012), 19, Kindle.
29. Ibid., 41.
30. Ibid., 47.
31. Ibid., 48.
32. Ibid.
33. Ibid., 105–6.
34. John G. Sotos, MD, "Taft and Pickwick: Sleep Apnea in the White House," *CHEST* 124, no. 3 (Sept. 2003): 1133, http://dx.doi.org /10.1378/chest.124.3.1133.
35. Ibid., 1135.
36. Ibid., 1138.
37. Ibid., 1137.
38. Lurie, *Taft: Travails of a Progressive Conservative*, 63 n.115.
39. William Howard Taft, "He Who Conquers Himself Is Greater than He Who Taketh a City," Address at Union Religious Service in Fresno City Hall Park, Oct. 10, 1909, in *The Collected Works of William Howard Taft*, vol. 3, 264.
40. Ibid.
41. Ibid., 266.
42. Lurie, *Taft: Travails of a Progressive Conservative*, x–xi.

1: "A JUDICIAL TEMPERAMENT"

1. Lewis Alexander Leonard, *Life of Alphonso Taft* (New York: Hawke, 1920), 20.
2. "Republican Party Platform of 1856," June 18, 1856, American Presidency Project, http://www.presidency.ucsb.edu/ws/?pid=29619 [https://perma.cc/P5EU-677Z].
3. James Chace, *1912: Wilson, Roosevelt, and Debs—The Election That Changed the Country* (New York: Simon & Schuster Paperbacks, 2004), 23–24.

4. Doris Kearns Goodwin, *The Bully Pulpit: Theodore Roosevelt, William Howard Taft, and the Golden Age of Journalism* (New York: Simon & Schuster Paperbacks, 2013), 24.

5. Visit by author to William Howard Taft National Historic Site, Cincinnati, OH, July 7, 2017.

6. Minor v. Cincinnati Bd. of Education (Cincinnati Superior Ct. 1870), Opinion of Judge Storer, in *The Bible in the Public Schools. Arguments in the Case of J. D. Minor Versus The Board of Education of the City of Cincinnati* (Cincinnati: R. Clarke, 1870), 379.

7. Ibid., Opinion of Judge Taft, 390.

8. Abington School District v. Schempp, 374 U.S. 203 (1963).

9. Henry F. Pringle, *The Life and Times of William Howard Taft*, vol. 1 (Norwalk, CT: Easton Press, 1986), 45.

10. Jonathan Lurie, *William Howard Taft: The Travails of a Progressive Conservative* (New York: Cambridge University Press, 2012), 5.

11. Pringle, *Taft*, vol. 1, 73–74.

12. Ibid., 22.

13. Ibid., 35.

14. Judith Icke Anderson, *William Howard Taft: An Intimate History* (New York: W. W. Norton, 1981), 43; Leonard, *Alphonso Taft*, 29.

15. Bob Dellinger, *Wrestling in the USA*, National Wrestling Hall of Fame, http://nwhof.org/stillwater/resources-library/history/wrestling-in-the-usa/ [https://perma.cc/6CR9-EW3M].

16. "When Taft Was at Yale," *Index* 18, no. 5 (Feb. 1, 1908): 6.

17. Ishbel Ross, *An American Family: The Tafts* (1678–1964) (Santa Barbara, CA: Greenwood Press, 1977), 67.

18. Pringle, *Taft*, vol. 1, 47.

19. Goodwin, *Bully Pulpit*, 54–55.

20. Ibid., 55.

21. Ibid.

22. Pringle, *Taft*, vol. 1, 61.

23. Goodwin, *Bully Pulpit*, 56.

24. Ibid., 60.

25. Lurie, *Taft: Travails of a Progressive Conservative*, 15.

26. *The Literary Club of Cincinnati 1849–1903: Constitution, Catalogue of Members, Etc.* (Cincinnati: Ebbert & Richardson, 1903), 30.

27. Helen Herron Taft, *Recollections of Full Years* (New York: Dodd, Mead, 1914), 3, https://archive.org/details/recollectionsfu02taftgoog.

28. Ibid., 6.

29. Ibid.

30. Carl Sferrazza Anthony, *Nellie Taft: The Unconventional First Lady of the Ragtime Era* (New York: HarperCollins, 2005), 32.
31. Goodwin, *Bully Pulpit*, 89.
32. Anthony, *Nellie Taft*, 58.
33. Ibid., 69.
34. Ibid.
35. Ibid., 74–75.
36. Ibid., 75–76.
37. Lurie, *Taft: Travails of a Progressive Conservative*, 15.
38. Pringle, *Taft*, vol. 1, 82.
39. Helen Herron Taft, *Recollections*, 22.
40. Lurie, *Taft: Travails of a Progressive Conservative*, 23.
41. Thomas v. Cincinnati, N.O. & T.P. Railway Co., In re Phelan, 62 F. 803 (1894).
42. "George Mortimer Pullman," Pullman State Historic Site, June 2016, http://www.pullman-museum.org/theMan/ [https://perma .cc/U2M8-RRHC].
43. Lurie, *Taft: Travails of a Progressive Conservative*, 31.
44. Ibid.
45. Letter from William Howard Taft to Helen H. Taft, July 6, 1894, in Pringle, *Taft*, vol. 1, 128.
46. Lurie, *Taft: Travails of a Progressive Conservative*, 32.
47. Goodwin, *Bully Pulpit*, 215–16.
48. Lurie, *Taft: Travails of a Progressive Conservative*, 24.
49. Peri E. Arnold, *Remaking the Presidency: Roosevelt, Taft, and Wilson, 1901–1916* (Lawrence: University Press of Kansas, 2009), 75.
50. Goodwin, *Bully Pulpit*, 143–44.
51. Anderson, *Taft: An Intimate History*, 60.
52. Neal Kumar Katyal, "The Solicitor General and Confession of Error," *Fordham Law Review* 81 (2013): 3027, 3030.
53. Pringle, *Taft*, vol. 1, 16.
54. Goodwin, *Bully Pulpit*, 145–46.
55. Ibid., 145.
56. Arnold, *Remaking the Presidency*, 76.
57. Ibid.
58. Goodwin, *Bully Pulpit*, 152.
59. Pringle, *Taft*, vol. 1, 109.
60. Ibid., 122.
61. "William Taft: Life Before the Presidency," Miller Center, University of Virginia, http://millercenter.org/president/biography/taft -life-before-the-presidency [https://perma.cc/WZ45-FHRN].
62. Helen Herron Taft, *Recollections*, 30.

63. Anderson, *Taft: An Intimate History*, 64.
64. Pringle, *Taft*, vol. 1, 143.
65. 156 U.S. 1 (1895).
66. United States v. Addyston Pipe & Steel Co., 85 F. 271 (6th Cir. 1898).
67. Goodwin, *Bully Pulpit*, 218.
68. Addyston Pipe & Steel Co. v. United States, 175 U.S. 211 (1899). See also William Howard Taft, "Mr. Bryan's Claim to the Roosevelt Policies," Address in Sandusky, Ohio, Sept. 8, 1908, in *The Collected Works of William Howard Taft*, vol. 2, ed. David H. Burton (Athens: Ohio University Press, 2001), 47.
69. *Addyston*, 175 U.S. at 212.
70. Taft, "Mr. Bryan's Claim to the Roosevelt Policies," 48.
71. William Howard Taft, "The Railroads and the Courts," Address Delivered at Orchestra Hall in Chicago, Sept. 23, 1908, in *The Collected Works of William Howard Taft*, vol. 2, 91.
72. Ibid., 90.

2: "WE WANT TAFT"

1. Henry F. Pringle, *The Life and Times of William Howard Taft*, vol. 1 (Norwalk, CT: Easton Press, 1986), 159.
2. Ibid.
3. Ibid., 160.
4. Ibid.
5. Judith Icke Anderson, *William Howard Taft: An Intimate History* (New York: W. W. Norton, 1981), 66.
6. Pringle, *Taft*, vol. 1, 161.
7. Peri E. Arnold, *Remaking the Presidency: Roosevelt, Taft, and Wilson, 1901–1916* (Lawrence: University Press of Kansas, 2009), 80.
8. Jonathan Lurie, *William Howard Taft: The Travails of a Progressive Conservative* (New York: Cambridge University Press, 2012), 40.
9. Pringle, *Taft*, vol. 1, 161.
10. Helen Herron Taft, *Recollections of Full Years* (New York: Dodd, Mead, 1914), 35, https://archive.org/details/recollectionsfu02taftgoog.
11. Pringle, *Taft*, vol. 1, 165.
12. Ibid., 169. Arthur MacArthur's son, General Douglas MacArthur, would display similar insolence to civilian authorities in the Far East, keeping President Harry Truman waiting before greeting the president when he arrived for a meeting on Wake Island during the Korean War.
13. Lurie, *Taft: Travails of a Progressive Conservative*, 46.

14. Doris Kearns Goodwin, *The Bully Pulpit: Theodore Roosevelt, William Howard Taft, and the Golden Age of Journalism* (New York: Simon & Schuster Paperbacks, 2013), 274.

15. Helen Herron Taft, *Recollections*, 212.

16. John W. Grant, "William Howard Taft on America and the Philippines: Equality, Natural Rights, and Imperialism," in Joseph W. Postell and Johnathan O'Neill, *Toward an American Conservatism: Constitutional Conservatism During the Progressive Era* (New York: Palgrave Macmillan, 2013), 135, Kindle.

17. Ibid., 137–38.

18. Ibid., 129–33.

19. Ibid., 131.

20. Ibid., 133.

21. William Howard Taft, "Inaugural Address as Civil Governor of the Philippines," Address Before the Filipino People in Manila, July 4, 1901, in *The Collected Works of William Howard Taft*, vol. 1, ed. David H. Burton and A. E. Campbell (Athens: Ohio University Press, 2001), 75.

22. Helen Herron Taft, *Recollections*, 112.

23. Goodwin, *Bully Pulpit*, 269.

24. Pringle, *Taft*, vol. 1, 174.

25. Helen Herron Taft, *Recollections*, 217.

26. Arnold, *Remaking the Presidency*, 82.

27. Ibid., 84.

28. Pringle, *Taft*, vol. 1, 182.

29. William Howard Taft, "The Inauguration of Philippine Assembly," Address Before the Philippine Assembly, October 16, 1907, in *The Collected Works of William Howard Taft*, vol. 1, 92.

30. Helen Herron Taft, *Recollections*, 159.

31. Ibid.

32. Goodwin, *Bully Pulpit*, 272.

33. Pringle, *Taft*, vol. 1, 199.

34. Ibid., 191.

35. Ibid., 240.

36. Ibid., 241.

37. Helen Herron Taft, *Recollections*, 265.

38. Pringle, *Taft*, vol. 1, 243.

39. Ibid., 219.

40. Ibid.

41. Ibid., 223–31.

42. Ibid., 231.

43. Anderson, *Taft: An Intimate History*, 81.

44. Pringle, *Taft*, vol. 1, 245.
45. Helen Herron Taft, *Recollections*, 267.
46. Pringle, *Taft*, vol. 1, 247.
47. Ibid., 252.
48. Ibid.
49. Ibid., 254.
50. Goodwin, *Bully Pulpit*, 298.
51. Ibid., 299.
52. Ibid.
53. Northern Securities Co. v. United States, 193 U.S. 197 (1904).
54. Goodwin, *Bully Pulpit*, 399.
55. Pringle, *Taft*, vol. 1, 272.
56. Arnold, *Remaking the Presidency*, 89.
57. Pringle, *Taft*, vol. 1, 264.
58. Ibid., 309–10.
59. Frederick Palmer, "Taft, The Proconsul," *Collier's* 39 (April 13, 1907): 13.
60. Pringle, *Taft*, vol. 1, 276.
61. Ibid., 286.
62. Ibid., 286–88.
63. Andrew Dolan, *The Taft Diet: How President Taft Lost 76 Pounds* (CreateSpace Independent Publishing Platform, 2012), 28, Kindle.
64. Pringle, *Taft*, vol. 1, 288.
65. Alpheus Thomas Mason, *William Howard Taft: Chief Justice* (New York: Simon & Schuster, 1965), 30.
66. James Chace, *1912: Wilson, Roosevelt, and Debs—The Election That Changed the Country* (New York: Simon & Schuster Paperbacks, 2004), 26.
67. Ibid., 27.
68. Goodwin, *Bully Pulpit*, 535.
69. Ibid., 545.
70. Ibid., 546.
71. Henry Beach Needham, "Why the President Is for Taft," *Success Magazine* 11, no. 173 (Oct. 1908): 661.
72. William Howard Taft, "Speech of Acceptance Delivered at Cincinnati, Ohio," July 28, 1908, in *The Collected Works of William Howard Taft*, vol. 3, ed. David H. Burton (Athens: Ohio University Press, 2002), 7.
73. Goodwin, *Bully Pulpit*, 551.
74. Edgar A. Hornig, "Campaign Issues in the Presidential Election of 1908," *Indiana Magazine of History* 54, no. 3 (1958): 237–64.

75. "1908 Democratic Party Platform," July 7, 1908, American Presidency Project, http://www.presidency.ucsb.edu/ws/?pid=29589 [https://perma.cc/8QBB-LV8E].
76. Taft, "Speech of Acceptance," 14.
77. "Republican Party Platform of 1908," June 16, 1908, American Presidency Project, http://www.presidency.ucsb.edu/ws/?pid =29632 [https://perma.cc/437D-VU69].
78. Michael Kazin, *A Godly Hero: The Life of William Jennings Bryan* (New York: Anchor Books, 2007), 155.
79. Taft, "Speech of Acceptance," 19.
80. "1908 Democratic Party Platform," July 7, 1908.
81. Taft, "Speech of Acceptance," 35.
82. Anderson, *Taft: An Intimate History*, 93.
83. Goodwin, *Bully Pulpit*, 550.
84. Anderson, *Taft: An Intimate History*, 94.
85. *The Library of Congress Presents: Historic Presidential Speeches, 1908–1993*, Rhino Records, 1995, 6 CDs.
86. William Jennings Bryan, "Cross of Gold" Speech (1896, 1921), YouTube, https://www.youtube.com/watch?v=UV2wRCc WJa8.
87. William Howard Taft, "Republican Responsibility and Performance; Democratic Responsibility and Failure," *In Their Own Voices: The U.S. Presidential Elections of 1908–1912*, vol. 1, Marston Records 2000, recorded August 27, 1908, https://www.marstonrecords.com/products/voices#1-23 [https://perma.cc/5TCE-285C].
88. William Howard Taft, "Functions of the Next Administration," *In Their Own Voices*, vol. 1, recorded Aug. 5, 1908.
89. Pringle, *Taft*, vol. 1, 377.
90. Goodwin, *Bully Pulpit*, 556.

3: "THE BEST TARIFF BILL"

1. James Chace, *1912: Wilson, Roosevelt, and Debs—The Election That Changed the Country* (New York: Simon & Schuster Paperbacks, 2004), 13.
2. Helen Herron Taft, *Recollections of Full Years* (New York: Dodd, Mead, 1914), 326–27, https://archive.org/details/recollectionsfu02taftgoog.
3. Ibid., 327.
4. Ibid., 328.

5. Judith Icke Anderson, *William Howard Taft: An Intimate History* (New York: W. W. Norton, 1981), 119.
6. Doris Kearns Goodwin, *The Bully Pulpit: Theodore Roosevelt, William Howard Taft, and the Golden Age of Journalism* (New York: Simon & Schuster Paperbacks, 2013), 569.
7. Anderson, *Taft: An Intimate History*, 120.
8. Helen Herron Taft, *Recollections*, 330.
9. William Howard Taft, "Inaugural Address," Mar. 4, 1909, in *The Collected Works of William Howard Taft*, vol. 3, ed. David H. Burton (Athens: Ohio University Press, 2002), 45.
10. "Republican Party Platform of 1908," June 16, 1908, American Presidency Project, http://www.presidency.ucsb.edu/ws/?pid=29632 [https://perma.cc/B325-FYEA].
11. William Howard Taft, "A Pledge of Tariff Reform," Address Delivered in Milwaukee, Sept. 24, 1908, in *The Collected Works of William Howard Taft*, vol. 2, ed. David H. Burton (Athens: Ohio University Press, 2001), 105.
12. Taft, "Inaugural Address," 46.
13. Ibid.
14. Ibid.
15. Lewis L. Gould, *The William Howard Taft Presidency* (Lawrence: University Press of Kansas, 2009), 50.
16. William Howard Taft, "Message to Congress at the Second Session of the Sixty-First Congress," Dec. 7, 1909, in *The Collected Works of William Howard Taft*, vol. 3, 369.
17. Ibid., 370–71.
18. Sidney M. Milkis, "William Howard Taft and the Struggle for the Constitution," in Joseph W. Postell and Johnathan O'Neill, *Toward an American Conservatism: Constitutional Conservatism During the Progressive Era* (New York: Palgrave Macmillan, 2013), 68, Kindle.
19. Helen Herron Taft, *Recollections*, 331.
20. Pringle, *Taft*, vol. 1, 400–401.
21. Ibid., 401.
22. Ibid.
23. Helen Herron Taft, *Recollections*, 332–33.
24. Ibid., 346.
25. Gould, *William Howard Taft Presidency*, 33.
26. Lawrence F. Abbott, ed., *Taft and Roosevelt: The Intimate Letters of Archie Butt, Military Aide*, vol. 1 (Garden City, NY: Doubleday, Doran, 1930), 9.
27. William Howard Taft, "A Few Words to Southern Democrats,"

Address Delivered in Augusta, GA, Jan. 14, 1909, in *The Collected Works of William Howard Taft*, vol. 2, 170.

28. Pringle, *Taft*, vol. 1, 384.

29. Jonathan Lurie, *William Howard Taft: The Travails of a Progressive Conservative* (New York: Cambridge University Press, 2012), 91.

30. Goodwin, *Bully Pulpit*, 561–62.

31. Pringle, *Taft*, vol. 1, 387.

32. Ibid.

33. Lurie, *Taft: Travails of a Progressive Conservative*, 95.

34. Abbott, *Letters of Archie Butt*, vol. 1, 37.

35. Lawrence F. Abbott, ed., *Taft and Roosevelt: The Intimate Letters of Archie Butt, Military Aide*, vol. 2 (Garden City, NY: Doubleday, Doran, 1930), 659.

36. Abbott, *Letters of Archie Butt*, vol. 1, 37.

37. Gould, *William Howard Taft Presidency*, 45.

38. Goodwin, *Bully Pulpit*, 588.

39. William Howard Taft, "Message Convening Congress in Extra Session," Mar. 16, 1909, in *The Collected Works of William Howard Taft*, vol. 3, 56.

40. Ibid., 57.

41. William Howard Taft, "Address to Congress Concerning Tax on Net Income of Corporations," June 16, 1909, in *The Collected Works of William Howard Taft*, vol. 3, 133.

42. Goodwin, *Bully Pulpit*, 583. Although "Roosevelt had sympathized with progressive claims that high tariffs strengthened monopolies and artificially inflated prices." Ibid.

43. John Steele Gordon, *Hamilton's Blessing: The Extraordinary Life and Times of Our National Debt* (New York: Penguin Books, 1998), 23.

44. Ibid., 75–76.

45. Sheldon D. Pollack, "The First National Income Tax, 1861–1872," *Tax Lawyer* 67, no. 2 (2014): 5, http://udel.edu/~pollack/Down loaded%20SDP%20articles,%20etc/academic%20articles/The%20 First%20National%20Income%20Tax%2012-18-2013.pdf [https:// perma.cc/8PNU-S2L2].

46. Pollock v. Farmers' Loan & Trust Co., 157 U.S. 429 (1895).

47. "Income Tax," Interactive Constitution, National Constitution Center, https://constitutioncenter.org/interactive-constitution /amendments/amendment-xvi [https://perma.cc/WX3Q-Z8RW].

48. William Howard Taft, "The Achievements of the Republican Party," Address Before the Young Men's Republican Club of Missouri, Kansas City, Feb. 10, 1908, *Present Day Problems*, in *The*

Collected Works of William Howard Taft, vol. 1, ed. David H. Burton and A. E. Campbell (Athens: Ohio University Press, 2001), 286.

49. Paul Wolman, *Most Favored Nation: The Republican Revisionists and U.S. Tariff Policy* (Chapel Hill: University of North Carolina Press, 1992), xi–xii.
50. Chace, *1912*, 33.
51. Michael Nelson, ed., *Guide to the Presidency and Executive Branch*, 5th ed. (Thousand Oaks, CA: CQ Press, 2012), 126.
52. Anderson, *Taft: An Intimate History*, 140.
53. Wolman, *Most Favored Nation*, 145.
54. Ibid.; Gould, *William Howard Taft Presidency*, 54.
55. Wolman, *Most Favored Nation*, 147.
56. Gould, *William Howard Taft Presidency*, 54–55.
57. Anderson, *Taft: An Intimate History*, 155.
58. Abbott, *Letters of Archie Butt*, vol. 2, 638.
59. Pringle, *Taft*, vol. 1, 443.
60. Helen Herron Taft, *Recollections*, 365.
61. Abbott, *Letters of Archie Butt*, vol. 1, 88.
62. Anderson, *Taft: An Intimate History*, 167.
63. Abbott, *Letters of Archie Butt*, vol. 2, 650.
64. Anderson, *Taft: An Intimate History*, 171.
65. Letter from William Howard Taft to Nellie Taft (July 22, 1909), in Lewis L. Gould, ed., *My Dearest Nellie: The Letters of William Howard Taft to Helen Herron Taft (1909–1912)* (Lawrence: University Press of Kansas, 2011), 52–53.
66. Anderson, *Taft: An Intimate History*, 173.
67. Abbott, *Letters of Archie Butt*, vol. 1, 144.
68. Letter from William Howard Taft to Nellie Taft (July 30, 1909), in Gould, *My Dearest Nellie*, 61.
69. William Howard Taft, Address at the Lincoln Birthday Banquet of the Republican Club of New York, Feb. 12, 1910, in *The Collected Works of William Howard Taft*, vol. 3, 451–53.
70. Gould, *William Howard Taft Presidency*, 51.
71. Ibid., 60.
72. Anderson, *Taft: An Intimate History*, 173; Gould, *William Howard Taft Presidency*, 51.
73. Goodwin, *Bully Pulpit*, 594.
74. Taft, "Address to Congress Concerning Tax on Net Income of Corporations," 134.
75. Ibid., 135.
76. Ibid., 133.
77. Gordon, *Hamilton's Blessing*, 96–97.

78. William Howard Taft, "An Appreciation of General Grant," Speech Delivered in New York City, May 30, 1908, in *The Collected Works of William Howard Taft*, vol. 1, 125.

79. Ibid.

80. Pringle, *Taft*, vol. 1, 457.

81. Abbott, *Letters of Archie Butt*, vol. 1, 200.

82. Gould, *My Dearest Nellie*, 70.

83. William Howard Taft, "Address in Winona, Minnesota, on the Tariff," Sept. 17, 1909, in *The Collected Works of William Howard Taft*, vol. 3, 172.

84. Ibid., 177.

85. Anderson, *Taft: An Intimate History*, 175.

86. Sean Wilentz, *The Politicians and the Egalitarians: The Hidden History of American Politics* (New York: W. W. Norton, 2016).

87. Ibid., 179.

88. William Howard Taft, "Address in Denver on Corporation and Income Taxes," Sept. 21, 1909, in *The Collected Works of William Howard Taft*, vol. 3, 195.

89. Ibid., 201–202.

90. Ibid., 202.

91. Pringle, *Taft*, vol. 1, 459.

92. Ibid., 461.

93. Ibid., 462.

94. Ibid., 465.

95. William Howard Taft, "Address at Georgia State Fair Grounds on Wisdom and Necessity of Following the Law," Nov. 4, 1909, in *The Collected Works of William Howard Taft*, vol. 3, 323.

96. Ibid., 324.

4: "WITHIN THE LAW"

1. Sidney M. Milkis, "William Howard Taft and the Struggle for the Constitution," in Joseph W. Postell and Johnathan O'Neill, *Toward an American Conservatism: Constitutional Conservatism During the Progressive Era* (New York: Palgrave Macmillan, 2013), 69, Kindle.

2. Doris Kearns Goodwin, *The Bully Pulpit: Theodore Roosevelt, William Howard Taft, and the Golden Age of Journalism* (New York: Simon & Schuster Paperbacks, 2013), 606.

3. Ibid.

4. Peri E. Arnold, *Remaking the Presidency: Roosevelt, Taft, and Wilson, 1901–1916* (Lawrence: University Press of Kansas, 2009), 119.

5. Judith Icke Anderson, *William Howard Taft: An Intimate History* (New York: W. W. Norton, 1981), 181.

6. Milkis, "Taft and the Struggle for the Constitution," 70.
7. Ibid.
8. Ibid.
9. Jonathan Lurie, *William Howard Taft: The Travails of a Progressive Conservative* (New York: Cambridge University Press, 2012), 160.
10. Goodwin, *Bully Pulpit*, 606.
11. Henry F. Pringle, *The Life and Times of William Howard Taft*, vol. 1 (Norwalk, CT: Easton Press, 1986), 478.
12. Arnold, *Remaking the Presidency*, 118.
13. Pringle, *Taft*, vol. 1, 500–501.
14. Ibid., 121–22.
15. Lurie, *Taft: Travails of a Progressive Conservative*, 110; Goodwin, *Bully Pulpit*, 613.
16. Lawrence F. Abbott, ed., *Taft and Roosevelt: The Intimate Letters of Archie Butt, Military Aide*, vol. 1 (Garden City, NY: Doubleday, Doran, 1930), 193.
17. Ibid., 194.
18. Lurie, *Taft: Travails of a Progressive Conservative*, 110.
19. Arnold, *Remaking the Presidency*, 122.
20. Ibid.; Anderson, *Taft: An Intimate History*, 182.
21. Letter from William Howard Taft to Helen Herron Taft, Oct. 3, 1909, in Lewis L. Gould, ed., *My Dearest Nellie: Letters of William Howard Taft to Helen Herron Taft (1909–1912)* (Lawrence: University Press of Kansas, 2011), 73.
22. Ibid.
23. William Howard Taft, "Address at a Dallas Banquet on Conservation of National Resources and Irrigation," Oct. 23, 1909, in *The Collected Works of William Howard Taft*, vol. 3, ed. David H. Burton (Athens: Ohio University Press, 2002), 302.
24. Lewis L. Gould, *The William Howard Taft Presidency* (Lawrence: University Press of Kansas, 2009), 71.
25. Pringle, *Taft*, vol. 1, 480.
26. Abbott, *Letters of Archie Butt*, vol. 1, 208.
27. Arnold, *Remaking the Presidency*, 122.
28. Pringle, *Taft*, vol. 1, 472.
29. Gould, *William Howard Taft Presidency*, 72–73.
30. Ibid., 74; Arnold, *Remaking the Presidency*, 124–25.
31. Melvin I. Urofsky, *Louis D. Brandeis: A Life* (New York: Pantheon Books, 2009), 258–60.
32. Abbott, *Letters of Archie Butt*, vol. 1, 203.
33. Ibid., 245.
34. Gould, *William Howard Taft Presidency*, 75.
35. Ibid.

36. Abbott, *Letters of Archie Butt*, vol. 1, 254.
37. William Howard Taft, "Address to Congress on Conservation of National Resources," Jan. 14, 1910, in *The Collected Works of William Howard Taft*, vol. 3, 428.
38. "Can This Be Whitewashed Also?," *San Francisco Call*, Dec. 17, 1909, http://chroniclingamerica.loc.gov/lccn/sn85066387/1909 -12-17/ed-1/seq-6.pdf [https://perma.cc/YSC6-QQX7].
39. Milkis, "Taft and the Struggle for the Constitution," 71.
40. Arnold, *Remaking the Presidency*, 126.
41. Ibid., 127.
42. Anderson, *Taft: An Intimate History*, 184.
43. Ibid.
44. Letter from William Howard Taft to Knute Nelson (May 15, 1910), in "Investigation of the Dep't of the Interior and of the Bureau of Forestry," 61st Cong., Report of Commission (1911): 60, 62.
45. Ibid., 61.
46. Ibid., 62.
47. Ibid.
48. Goodwin, *Bully Pulpit*, 623.
49. Ibid., 626.
50. Milkis, "Taft and the Struggle for the Constitution," 73.
51. Anderson, *Taft: An Intimate History*, 184.
52. Ibid.
53. Abbott, *Letters of Archie Butt*, vol. 1, 298.
54. James Chace, *1912: Wilson, Roosevelt, and Debs—The Election That Changed the Country* (New York: Simon & Schuster Paperbacks, 2004), 17.
55. Ibid., 11.
56. Gould, *William Howard Taft Presidency*, 76; Lurie, *Taft: Travails of a Progressive Conservative*, 116.
57. Abbott, *Letters of Archie Butt*, vol. 1, 411.
58. Ibid., 497.
59. Ibid., 436.
60. Ibid., 482.
61. Chace, *1912*, 57.
62. Theodore Roosevelt, "New Nationalism Speech," Aug. 31, 1910, Ashbrook Center, Ashland University, http://teachingamerican history.org/library/document/new-nationalism-speech// [https:// perma.cc/9E2L-22EU].
63. William Howard Taft, "Mr. Bryan's Claim to the Roosevelt Policies," Address in Sandusky, Ohio, Sept. 8, 1908, in *The Collected Works of William Howard Taft*, vol. 2, ed. David H. Burton (Athens: Ohio University Press 2001), 46.

64. Ibid., 44.
65. Ibid., 48.
66. "The Mann-Elkins Act, Amending the Act to Regulate Commerce," *Quarterly Journal of Economics* (Aug. 1910), https://archive.org/stream/jstor-1883490/1883490_djvu.txt [https://perma.cc/QE8U-9XPQ].
67. William Howard Taft, "Address to Congress on Interstate Commerce and Anti-Trust Laws and Federal Incorporation," Jan. 7, 1910, in *The Collected Works of William Howard Taft*, vol. 3, 409–10.
68. Ibid., 417.
69. Ibid., 418.
70. 156 U.S. 1 (1895).
71. Taft, "Address to Congress on Interstate Commerce and Anti-Trust Laws," 419.
72. Ibid., 422.
73. Henry F. Pringle, *The Life and Times of William Howard Taft*, vol. 2 (Norwalk, CT: Easton Press, 1986), 660.
74. Ibid., 663.
75. Standard Oil of New Jersey v. United States, 221 U.S. 1 (1911).
76. Anderson, *Taft: An Intimate History*, 199.
77. *Standard Oil*, 221 U.S. at 97–98 (Harlan, J., concurring in part and dissenting in part).
78. United States v. American Tobacco Co., 221 U.S. 106, 180–81 (1911).
79. Pringle, *Taft*, vol. 2, 665.
80. Ibid., 666.
81. Jonathan P. Hicks, "U.S. Steel: New Name Ends an Era," *New York Times*, July 9, 1986, http://www.nytimes.com/1986/07/09/business/us-steel-new-name-ends-an-era.html?mcubz=1 [https://perma.cc/9VHW-FFD8].
82. Goodwin, *Bully Pulpit*, 297–98.
83. Ibid., 667.
84. Pringle, *Taft*, vol. 2, 670.
85. Theodore Roosevelt, "The Trusts, The People and the Square Deal," *Outlook*, Nov. 18, 1911, http://www.theodore-roosevelt.com/images/research/treditorials/o65.pdf [https://perma.cc/2LXL-4CNM].
86. Goodwin, *Bully Pulpit*, 668.
87. Gould, *William Howard Taft Presidency*, 165–67.
88. Lawrence F. Abbott, ed., *Taft and Roosevelt: The Intimate Letters of Archie Butt, Military Aide*, vol. 2 (Garden City, NY: Doubleday, Doran, 1930), 813.

89. Roosevelt, "The Trusts."

90. William Kolasky, "The Election of 1912: A Pivotal Moment in Antitrust History, *Antitrust* 25, no. 3 (2011): 82, 83, http://www.wilmerhale.com/uploadedFiles/WilmerHale_Shared _Content/Files/Editorial/Publication/The%20Election%20 of%201912%20-%20Kolasky.pdf [https://perma.cc/G2FC-4FYF].

91. William Howard Taft, "Annual Message Part I, Address Before Congress on the Anti-Trust Statute," Dec. 5, 1911, in *The Collected Works of William Howard Taft*, vol. 4, ed. David H. Burton (Athens: Ohio University Press, 2002), 162.

92. Ibid., 166–67.

93. Pringle, *Taft*, vol. 2, 657.

94. Ibid., 676.

95. Anderson, *Taft: An Intimate History*, 204.

96. Pringle, *Taft*, vol. 2, 678.

97. David H. Burton, *William Howard Taft: Confident Peacemaker* (Philadelphia: Saint Joseph's University Press, 2004), 72.

98. Ibid.

99. Abbott, *Letters of Archie Butt*, vol. 2, 645.

100. Ibid., 733.

101. William Howard Taft, "Annual Message Part II," Address Before Congress on Foreign Relations, Dec. 7, 1911, in *The Collected Works of William Howard Taft*, vol. 4, 177.

102. Ibid.

103. Ibid., 180.

104. Burton, *Confident Peacemaker*, 73.

105. Chris Edelson, *Emergency Presidential Power: From the Drafting of the Constitution to the War on Terror* (Madison: University of Wisconsin Press, 2013), 29.

106. William Howard Taft, *The President and His Powers*, in *The Collected Works of William Howard Taft*, vol. 6, ed. W. Carey McWilliams and Frank X. Gerrity (Athens: Ohio University Press 2003), 107. (Originally published in 1916 as *Our Chief Magistrate and His Powers*.)

107. Ibid.

108. Jean West Mueller and Wynell B. Schamel, "Lincoln's Spot Resolutions," *Social Education* 52 (Oct. 1988): 455–457, 466.

109. Burton, *Confident Peacemaker*, 63.

110. Ibid., 78.

111. William Howard Taft, "Special Message on Canadian Reciprocity," Jan. 26, 1911, in *The Collected Works of William Howard Taft*, vol. 4, 109–10.

112. William Howard Taft, "Proclamation of March 4, 1911," Address

Before Extra Session of Congress to Consider Canadian-American Tariff Agreement, Mar. 4, 1911, in *The Collected Works of William Howard Taft*, vol. 4, 113–14.

113. William Howard Taft, "Special Message," Address to Congress on the Reciprocal Tariff Agreement between the Dominion of Canada and the United States, Apr. 5, 1911, in *The Collected Works of William Howard Taft*, vol. 4, 115.

114. Pringle, *Taft*, vol. 2, 593.

115. Abbott, *Letters of Archie Butt*, vol. 2, 710.

116. Burton, *Confident Peacemaker*, 79.

117. "Making Canada an Adjunct," *Literary Digest* 44 (1912): 1029, http://www.unz.org/Pub/LiteraryDigest-1912may18-01029 [https://perma.cc/3MUJ-7JN2].

118. Burton, *Confident Peacemaker*, 80.

119. Pringle, *Taft*, vol. 2, 599.

120. William Howard Taft, *Popular Government: Its Essence, Its Permanence, and Its Perils*, in *The Collected Works of William Howard Taft*, vol. 5, ed. David Potash and Donald F. Anderson (Athens: Ohio University Press, 2003), 157.

121. Pringle, *Taft*, vol. 2, 738.

122. Ibid.

123. Burton, *Confident Peacemaker*, 82.

124. "William Howard Taft—Foreign Affairs," Profiles of U.S. Presidents, http://www.presidentprofiles.com/Grant-Eisenhower /William-Howard-Taft-Foreign-affairs.html [https://perma .cc/ZLN3-P255].

125. Abbott, *Letters of Archie Butt*, vol. 2, 757.

126. Pringle, *Taft*, vol. 2, 749.

127. Abbott, *Letters of Archie Butt*, vol. 2, 804.

128. Burton, *Confident Peacemaker*, 82.

129. Anderson, *Taft: An Intimate History*, 197–98.

130. Pringle, *Taft*, vol. 2, 713.

131. Ibid., 715.

132. Ibid., 755.

5: "POPULAR UNREST"

1. Theodore Roosevelt, "A Charter for Democracy," Feb. 21, 1912, Ashbrook Center, Ashland University, http://teachingamerican history.org/library/document/a-charter-for-democracy// [https://perma.cc/6XJZ-XZF7].

2. Ibid.

3. James Chace, *1912: Wilson, Roosevelt, and Debs—The Election That Changed the Country* (New York: Simon & Schuster Paperbacks, 2004), 106.
4. Lawrence F. Abbott, ed., *Taft and Roosevelt: The Intimate Letters of Archie Butt, Military Aide*, vol. 2 (Garden City, NY: Doubleday, Doran, 1930), 850.
5. William Howard Taft, "Speech Delivered in Boston," Apr. 25, 1912, in 38 Senate Docs., 62nd Cong. (Dec. 4, 1911–Aug. 26, 1912): 3–4.
6. Ibid., 5.
7. Ibid., 19.
8. Lewis L. Gould, *The William Howard Taft Presidency* (Lawrence: University Press of Kansas, 2009), 177.
9. Henry F. Pringle, *The Life and Times of William Howard Taft*, vol. 2 (Norwalk, CT: Easton Press, 1986), 783.
10. Doris Kearns Goodwin, *The Bully Pulpit: Theodore Roosevelt, William Howard Taft, and the Golden Age of Journalism* (New York: Simon & Schuster Paperbacks, 2013), 696.
11. Gould, *William Howard Taft Presidency*, 161.
12. Chace, *1912*, 113.
13. Ibid., 116.
14. Ibid., 117.
15. Pringle, *Taft*, vol. 2, 802.
16. Jonathan Lurie, *William Howard Taft: The Travails of a Progressive Conservative* (New York: Cambridge University Press, 2012), 166.
17. Chace, *1912*, 121.
18. Pringle, *Taft*, vol. 2, 809.
19. Chace, *1912*, 123.
20. Pringle, *Taft*, vol. 2, 813.
21. Letter from William Howard Taft to Nellie Taft, July 15, 1912, in Lewis L. Gould, ed., *My Dearest Nellie: The Letters of William Howard Taft to Helen Herron Taft (1909–1912)* (Lawrence: University Press of Kansas, 2011), 209.
22. Pringle, *Taft*, vol. 2, 815.
23. Ibid., 816.
24. Ganesh Sitaraman, *The Crisis of the Middle-Class Constitution: Why Economic Inequality Threatens Our Republic* (New York: Alfred A. Knopf, 2017), 176–78.
25. Peri E. Arnold, *Remaking the Presidency: Roosevelt, Taft, and Wilson, 1901–1916* (Lawrence: University Press of Kansas, 2009), 161.

26. "Progressive Party Platform of 1912," Nov. 5, 1912, American Presidency Project, http://www.presidency.ucsb.edu/ws/?pid=29617 [https://perma.cc/8WUF-BUBE].

27. "Republican Party Platform of 1912," June 18, 1912, American Presidency Project http://www.presidency.ucsb.edu/ws/?pid=29633 [https://perma.cc/47D2-GNGJ].

28. "1912 Democratic Party Platform," June 25, 1912, American Presidency Project, http://www.presidency.ucsb.edu/ws/?pid=29590 [https://perma.cc/B2RL-Q4HJ].

29. *The Democratic Text-Book*, Democratic National Committee (1912): 2, https://hdl.handle.net/2027/mdp.39015030798477.

30. "Republican Party Platform of 1912."

31. "Progressive Party Platform of 1912."

32. Letter from William Howard Taft to Nellie Taft, July 16, 1912, in Gould, *My Dearest Nellie*, 211.

33. Letter from William Howard Taft to Nellie Taft, July 22, 1912, in Gould, *My Dearest Nellie*, 233–34.

34. Ibid., 234.

35. Letter from William Howard Taft to Nellie Taft, July 24, 1912, in Gould, *My Dearest Nellie*, 241.

36. "Speech Accepting the Nomination for the Presidency by the Republican National Committee," Aug. 1, 1912, in *The Republican Campaign Text-Book*, Republican National Committee (1912): 7, https://hdl.handle.net/2027/hvd.hw2hd8.

37. Ibid., 11.

38. Ibid.

39. Ibid.,12.

40. Ibid., 22.

41. Letter from William Howard Taft to Nellie Taft, July 16, 1912, in Gould, *My Dearest Nellie*, 211.

42. William Howard Taft, "Popular Unrest," *In Their Own Voices: The U.S. Presidential Elections of 1908–1912*, vol. 2, Marston Records 2000, recorded Oct. 1, 1912, https://www.marstonrecords.com/products/voices#1-23.

43. Judith Icke Anderson, *William Howard Taft: An Intimate History* (New York: W. W. Norton, 1981), 233.

44. Pringle, *Taft*, vol. 2, 838.

45. "1912 Presidential Election," 270toWin, http://www.270towin.com/1912_Election/ [https://perma.cc/8K73-GM7J].

46. Gould, *William Howard Taft Presidency*, 197.

47. Ibid.

48. Ibid., 202.

49. Mark Alden Branch, "Big Man on Campus," *Yale Alumni Magazine* (Mar./Apr. 2013), https://yalealumnimagazine.com/articles/3632 -big-man-on-campus.

50. William Howard Taft, "Annual Message Part III, Address to Congress on the Departments of the Post Office, Interior, Agriculture, and Commerce and Labor and District of Columbia," Dec. 19, 1912, in *The Collected Works of William Howard Taft*, vol. 4, ed. David H. Burton (Athens: Ohio University Press, 2002), 336.

51. "President Taft to Yale. Kent Professor-Elect Says He Is Happy to Return," *Yale Daily News* 36, no. 117 (Feb. 25, 1913), http://digital .library.yale.edu/cdm/compoundobject/collection/yale-ydn/id /93011/rec/1.

52. William Howard Taft, "Veto Message to the House of Representatives on H.R. 28775," Mar. 4, 1913, in *The Collected Works of William Howard Taft*, vol. 4, 366.

53. Pringle, *Taft*, vol. 2, 857.

54. Andrew Dolan, *The Taft Diet: How President Taft Lost 76 Pounds* (CreateSpace Independent Publishing Platform, 2012), 79, Kindle.

55. Allan B. Schwartz, "Medical Mystery: Who's Snoring in the White House?," *Philadelphia Inquirer*, Jan. 1, 2017, http://www.philly .com/philly/health/Medical-Mystery-Whos-Snoring-in-the -White-House—.html [https://perma.cc/3ZKF-CJGX].

56. John G. Sotos, MD, "Taft and Pickwick: Sleep Apnea in the White House," *CHEST* 124, no. 3 (Sept. 2003): 1137, http://dx.doi.org /10.1378/chest.124.3.1133.

57. David Potash, "Commentary," in *The Collected Works of William Howard Taft*, vol. 5, ed. David Potash and Donald F. Anderson (Athens: Ohio University Press 2003), 11.

58. William Howard Taft, *Popular Government: Its Essence, Its Permanence, and Its Perils*, in *The Collected Works of William Howard Taft*, vol. 5, 21.

59. Ibid.

60. Ibid., 37.

61. Ibid., 54.

62. Ibid., 57.

6: "I LOVE JUDGES AND I LOVE COURTS"

1. Lawrence F. Abbott, ed., *Taft and Roosevelt: The Intimate Letters of Archie Butt, Military Aide*, vol. 2 (Garden City, NY: Doubleday, Doran, 1930), 439.

2. Lawrence F. Abbott, ed., *Taft and Roosevelt: The Intimate Letters*

of Archie Butt, Military Aide, vol. 1 (Garden City, NY: Doubleday, Doran, 1930), 310.

3. Henry F. Pringle, *The Life and Times of William Howard Taft*, vol. 2 (Norwalk, CT: Easton Press, 1986), 955.

4. Ibid.

5. Ibid., 958.

6. Jonathan Lurie, *William Howard Taft: The Travails of a Progressive Conservative* (New York: Cambridge University Press, 2012), 197.

7. Robert Post, "Mr. Taft Becomes Chief Justice," *University of Cincinnati Law Review* 76 (2008): 761, 768–70.

8. Ibid., 777.

9. "Supreme Court Nominations: present–1789," U.S. Senate, https://www.senate.gov/pagelayout/reference/nominations/Nominations.htm [https://perma.cc/RF45-6VB6].

10. Pringle, *Taft*, vol. 2, 960.

11. Ibid., 965–66.

12. Ibid., 962.

13. Alpheus Thomas Mason, *William Howard Taft: Chief Justice* (New York: Simon & Schuster, 1965), 231.

14. Pringle, *Taft*, vol. 2, 972.

15. Ibid., 960.

16. Francis Graham Lee, "Commentary," in *The Collected Works of William Howard Taft*, vol. 8, ed. Francis Graham Lee (Athens: Ohio University Press, 2004), xvii.

17. Robert Post, "The Supreme Court Opinion as Institutional Practice: Dissent, Legal Scholarship, and Decisionmaking in the Taft Court," *Minnesota Law Review* 85 (2001): 1267, 1271.

18. Post, "Mr. Taft Becomes Chief Justice," 779–80.

19. Paolo E. Coletta, *The Presidency of William Howard Taft* (Lawrence: University Press of Kansas, 1973), 130.

20. Post, "Mr. Taft Becomes Chief Justice," 779.

21. Lee, "Commentary," in *The Collected Works of William Howard Taft*, vol. 8, xviii–xix.

22. "Landmark Legislation: Conference of Senior Circuit Judges," Stat. 42 (Sept. 14, 1922): 837, https://www.fjc.gov/history/legislation/landmark-judicial-legislation-text-document-12 [https://perma.cc/C2WE-3Q8Z].

23. Robert Post, "Judicial Management and Judicial Disinterest: The Achievements and Perils of Chief Justice William Howard Taft," *Journal of Supreme Court History* (1998): 54.

24. Ibid.

25. Ibid., 56.

26. Ibid.
27. Mason, *Taft: Chief Justice*, 56.
28. Ibid., 51.
29. Post, "The Supreme Court Opinion as Institutional Practice," 1384, app. A.
30. Ibid., 1278.
31. "Frequently Asked Questions (FAQ)," Supreme Court of the United States, https://www.supremecourt.gov/faq.aspx [https://perma.cc/6ZSK-6F28].
32. Post, "The Supreme Court Opinion as Institutional Practice," 1272–73.
33. Melvin I. Urofsky, *Louis D. Brandeis: A Life* (New York: Pantheon Books, 2009), 573.
34. Melvin I. Urofsky, *The Brandeis-Frankfurter Conversations*, *Supreme Court Review* 1985 (1985): 299, 313 (cited by Post, "Mr. Taft Becomes Chief Justice," 781).
35. Mason, *Taft: Chief Justice*, 199.
36. Robert Post, "Chief Justice William Howard Taft and the Concept of Federalism," *Constitutional Commentary* 9 (1992): 199, 202.
37. Abbott, *Letters of Archie Butt*, vol. 1, 293–94.
38. M. Todd Henderson, "From Seriatim to Consensus and Back Again: A Theory of Dissent," *Supreme Court Review 2007* (2007): 283, 325.
39. Post, "The Supreme Court Opinion as Institutional Practice," 1283.
40. Henderson, "A Theory of Dissent," 323.
41. Lee Epstein, William M. Landes, and Richard A. Posner, "Are Even Unanimous Decisions in the United States Supreme Court Ideological?," *Northwestern University Law Review* 106, no. 2 (2012): 699, 701.
42. Post, "Mr. Taft Becomes Chief Justice," 787.
43. Post, "The Supreme Court Opinion as Institutional Practice," 1311.
44. Mason, *Taft: Chief Justice*, 223.
45. Post, "The Supreme Court Opinion as Institutional Practice," 1311.
46. Ibid., 1344.
47. Ibid., 1343, n. 230.
48. Ibid., 1318–25.
49. Ibid., 1347.
50. Ibid., 1268.

51. Ibid., 1271.
52. Michael E. Parrish, *The Hughes Court: Justices, Rulings, and Legacy* (Santa Barbara, CA: ABC-CLIO, 2002), 23.
53. Lee, *The Collected Works of William Howard Taft*, vol. 8, 30.
54. Parrish, *The Hughes Court*, 23.
55. 259 U.S. 20 (1922) (Clarke, J., dissenting).
56. Alexander Bickel, *The Unpublished Opinions of Mr. Justice Brandeis: The Supreme Court at Work* (Cambridge, MA: Belknap Press, 1957), 19.
57. Bailey v. Drexel Furniture Co., 259 U.S. at 39 (citing Hammer v. Dagenhart, 247 U.S. 251 [1918]).
58. Ibid., 38.
59. Adkins v. Children's Hospital, 261 U.S. 525 (1923) (Taft, C.J., dissenting) (disapproving of the Court's upholding of *Lochner* and holding of a congressional act instituting minimum wage legislation for women invalid).
60. Ibid., 562 (Taft, C.J., dissenting).
61. Robert Post, "Federalism, Positive Law, and the Emergence of the American Administrative State: Prohibition in the Taft Court Era," *William & Mary Law Review* 48, no. 1 (2006): 87–88 (citing Letter from William Howard Taft to Allen B. Lincoln [Sept. 2, 1918]).
62. Pringle, *Taft*, vol. 2, 1077.
63. William Howard Taft, *The Citizen's Duty Under Prohibition* (Boston: Massachusetts Anti-Saloon League, 1919), 1.
64. 267 U.S. 132.
65. 272 U.S. 52.
66. Urofsky, *Brandeis: A Life*, 588.
67. *Myers*, 272 U.S. at 117.
68. Ibid., 134.
69. Ibid., 293 (Brandeis, J., dissenting).
70. 295 U.S. 602.
71. *Humphrey's Executor*, 295 U.S. at 629.
72. Christopher S. Yoo, Steven G. Calabresi, and Laurence D. Nee, "The Unitary Executive During the Third Half-Century, 1889–1945," Faculty Scholarship Paper No. 785 (2005): 43, http://scholarship.law.upenn.edu/faculty_scholarship/785.
73. Lee, *The Collected Works of William Howard Taft*, vol. 8, 258.
74. Yoo, Calabresi, and Nee, "The Unitary Executive," 42.
75. Taft, "Inaugural Address," 54.
76. Gong Lum v. Rice, 275 U.S. 78, 87 (1927).

77. John G. Sotos, MD, "Taft and Pickwick: Sleep Apnea in the White House," *CHEST* 124, no. 3 (2003): 1137.
78. Pringle, *Taft*, vol. 2, 1077.
79. Ibid., 1074.
80. Ibid.
81. Ibid., 1078.
82. Ibid., 1079.
83. Visit by author to U.S. Supreme Court, Washington, D.C., Apr. 19, 2017.
84. Mason, *Taft: Chief Justice*, 136–37.

EPILOGUE

1. Melvin I. Urofsky, *Brandeis: A Life* (New York: Pantheon Books, 2009), 572.
2. Peri E. Arnold, *Remaking the Presidency: Roosevelt, Taft, and Wilson, 1901–1916* (Lawrence: University Press of Kansas, 2009), 10.
3. Ibid., 108.
4. Letter from William Howard Taft to Nellie Taft, July 22, 1912, in Lewis L. Gould, ed., *My Dearest Nellie: The Letters of William Howard Taft to Helen Herron Taft* (1909–1912) (Lawrence: University Press of Kansas, 2011), 235.
5. Lawrence F. Abbott, ed., *Taft and Roosevelt: The Intimate Letters of Archie Butt, Military Aide*, vol. 2 (Garden City, NY: Doubleday, Doran, 1930), 593.
6. Lawrence F. Abbott, ed., *Taft and Roosevelt: The Intimate Letters of Archie Butt, Military Aide*, vol. 1 (Garden City, NY: Doubleday, Doran, 1930), 110–11.
7. W. Carey McWilliams, "Commentary," in *The Collected Works of William Howard Taft*, vol. 6, ed. W. Carey McWilliams and Frank X. Gerrity (Athens: Ohio University Press, 2003), 8.
8. William Howard Taft, "Veto Message Before the House of Representatives Returning Without Approval a Joint Resolution for Admission of New Mexico and Arizona into the Union as States," Aug. 22, 1911, in *The Collected Works of William Howard Taft*, vol. 4, ed. David H. Burton (Athens: Ohio University Press, 2002), 151–52.
9. William Howard Taft, *Liberty Under Law: An Interpretation of the Principles of Our Constitutional Government*, in *The Collected Works of William Howard Taft*, vol. 8, ed. Francis Graham Lee (Athens: Ohio University Press, 2004), 8.

10. Abbott, *Letters of Archie Butt*, vol. 1, 313–14.
11. Doris Kearns Goodwin, *The Bully Pulpit: Theodore Roosevelt, William Howard Taft, and the Golden Age of Journalism* (New York: Simon & Schuster Paperbacks, 2013), 736.
12. Abbott, *Letters of Archie Butt*, vol. 1, 201.
13. Ibid., vol. 2, 498.
14. Ibid., vol. 1, 38.
15. Ibid., 151.

Milestones

1857	Born in Cincinnati, Ohio, on September 15.
1878	Graduates from Yale second in his class; delivers senior oration as salutatorian. Enrolls in the University of Cincinnati Law School.
1880	Graduates from law school and passes the bar exam.
1880–1881	Works part-time as a reporter for the *Cincinnati Commercial Tribune*.
1881	Becomes assistant prosecutor of Hamilton County.
1882	Appointed collector of internal revenue in Cincinnati.
1883	Resigns as collector; works as an attorney in private practice.
1886	Marries Helen ("Nellie") Herron.
1887	Becomes a judge on the Ohio Superior Court.
1889	His son Robert Alphonso Taft is born.
1890	Appointed solicitor general of the United States.
1891	His father, Alphonso Taft, dies; his daughter, Helen Herron Taft, is born.
1892	Becomes a federal judge on the U.S. Court of Appeals for the Sixth Circuit.

1896	Named dean of the University of Cincinnati Law School. William McKinley is elected president.
1897	His son Charles Phelps Taft II is born.
1900	Named chairman of the Philippines Commission; arrives in Manila.
1901	Becomes civil governor of the Philippines. McKinley is assassinated, and Theodore Roosevelt becomes president. Declines appointment as an associate justice of the Supreme Court.
1902	Roosevelt declares the Philippine-American war over.
1903	Declines a second appointment as an associate justice of the Supreme Court.
1904	Becomes secretary of war. Visits Panama to oversee construction of the Panama Canal. Theodore Roosevelt is elected president in his own right.
1906	Serves temporarily as provisional governor of Cuba.
1907	His mother, Louisa Taft, dies.
1908	Accepts the Republican nomination for president and is elected the twenty-seventh president of the United States.
1909	Sworn in as president on March 4. Signs Payne-Aldrich Tariff Act. Appoints Horace Harmon Lurton to the Supreme Court. The Pinchot-Ballinger affair erupts.
1910	Roosevelt delivers his "New Nationalism" speech at Osawatomie, Kansas. Appoints Charles Evans Hughes, Willis Van Devanter, and Joseph Rucker Lamar to the Supreme Court and elevates Justice Edward Douglass White to be chief justice.
1911	Mobilizes twenty thousand American soldiers on the Mexican border.

Supreme Court orders dissolution of Standard Oil and
American Tobacco companies.
Signs Canadian Tariff Reciprocity Agreement, which
Canada rejects.
Signs arbitration treaties with France and England and
vetoes tariff reductions.
Taft administration files suit against U.S. Steel for
violating the Sherman Antitrust Act.

1912   Appoints Mahlon Pitney to the Supreme Court.
Is renominated by the Republican Party for president
during a bitter convention fight that splits the party.
Roosevelt forms the Progressive Party (also called the
Bull Moose Party) and runs as its candidate for president.
Sends marines to Cuba and Santo Domingo and battle-
ships to Nicaragua.
Woodrow Wilson wins presidential election, defeating
Taft and Roosevelt.

1913   The Sixteenth and Seventeenth Amendments are ratified.
Vetoes literacy tests for immigrants and the Webb-
Kenyon Interstate Liquor Act.
Leaves office and returns to Yale to teach law.
Publishes *Popular Government: Its Essence, Its Perma-
nence, and Its Perils*.

1914   Publishes *The Anti-Trust Act and the Supreme Court*.

1916   Publishes *Our Chief Magistrate and His Powers*.

1917   The United States declares war on Germany.

1918   Is named as co-chairman of the National War Labor
Board.
World War I ends.

1919   Theodore Roosevelt dies.
Eighteenth Amendment ratified, authorizing Prohibition.

1920   League of Nations founded.
Warren G. Harding is elected president.

1921   Appointed the tenth chief justice of the United States.

1922   Writes the opinions in *Stafford v. Wallace* and *Bailey v. Drexel Furniture Co.*
         Congress passes Conference of Senior Circuit Judges Act of 1922.
         Publishes *Liberty Under Law.*

1923   Issues a rare dissent in *Adkins v. Children's Hospital.*
         Harding dies in office; Calvin Coolidge becomes president.

1925   Congress passes the Judiciary Act of 1925.
         Writes the opinion in *Carroll v. United States.*

1926   Writes the opinion in *Myers v. United States.*

1927   Joins Justice Holmes's opinion in *Buck v. Bell.*

1928   Writes the opinion in *Olmstead v. United States.*
         Herbert Hoover elected president.

1929   After lobbying by Taft, Congress allocates funds for a new Supreme Court building.

1930   Resigns from the Supreme Court on February 3.
         Dies on March 8.

Selected Bibliography

Abbott, Lawrence F., ed. *Taft and Roosevelt: The Intimate Letters of Archie Butt, Military Aide.* 2 vols. Garden City, NY: Doubleday, Doran, 1930.

Anderson, Judith Icke. *William Howard Taft: An Intimate History.* New York: W. W. Norton, 1981.

Anthony, Carl Sferrazza. *Nellie Taft: The Unconventional First Lady of the Ragtime Era.* New York: HarperCollins, 2005.

Arnold, Peri E. *Remaking the Presidency: Roosevelt, Taft, and Wilson, 1901–1916.* Lawrence: University Press of Kansas, 2009.

Burton, David H. *William Howard Taft: Confident Peacemaker.* Philadelphia: Saint Joseph's University Press, 2004.

———, ed. *The Collected Works of William Howard Taft.* 8 vols. Athens: Ohio University Press, 2001–4.

Chace, James. *1912: Wilson, Roosevelt, and Debs—The Election That Changed the Country.* New York: Simon & Schuster Paperbacks, 2004.

Coletta, Paolo E. *The Presidency of William Howard Taft.* Lawrence: University Press of Kansas, 1973.

Dolan, Andrew. *The Taft Diet: How President Taft Lost 76 Pounds.* CreateSpace Independent Publishing Platform, 2012. Kindle.

Goodwin, Doris Kearns. *The Bully Pulpit: Theodore Roosevelt, William Howard Taft, and the Golden Age of Journalism.* New York: Simon & Schuster Paperbacks, 2013.

Gordon, John Steele. *Hamilton's Blessing: The Extraordinary Life and Times of Our National Debt.* New York: Penguin Books, 1998.

Gould, Lewis L. *The William Howard Taft Presidency.* Lawrence: University Press of Kansas, 2009.

———, ed. *My Dearest Nellie: The Letters of William Howard Taft to Helen Herron Taft (1909–1912)*. Lawrence: University Press of Kansas, 2011.

Leonard, Lewis Alexander. *Life of Alphonso Taft*. New York: Hawke, 1920.

Lurie, Jonathan. *William Howard Taft: The Travails of a Progressive Conservative*. New York: Cambridge University Press, 2014.

Mason, Alpheus Thomas. *William Howard Taft: Chief Justice*. New York: Simon & Schuster, 1965.

Postell, Joseph W., and Johnathan O'Neill. *Toward an American Conservatism: Constitutional Conservatism During the Progressive Era*. New York: Palgrave Macmillan, 2013. Kindle.

Pringle, Henry F. *The Life and Times of William Howard Taft*. 2 vols. Norwalk, CT: Easton Press, 1986.

Taft, Helen Herron. *Recollections of Full Years*. New York: Dodd, Mead, 1914. https://archive.org/details/recollectionsfu02taftgoog.

Taft, William Howard. *The Anti-Trust Act and the Supreme Court*, 1914. In *The Collected Works of William Howard Taft*. Vol. 5, edited by David Potash and Donald F. Anderson. Athens: Ohio University Press, 2003.

———. *Liberty Under Law*, 1922. In *The Collected Works of William Howard Taft*. Vol. 8, edited by Francis Graham Lee. Athens: Ohio University Press, 2004.

———. *Popular Government: Its Essence, Its Permanence, and Its Perils*, 1913. In *The Collected Works of William Howard Taft*. Vol. 5, edited by David Potash and Donald F. Anderson. Athens: Ohio University Press, 2003.

———. *Present Day Problems*, 1908. In *The Collected Works of William Howard Taft*. Vol. 1, edited by David H. Burton and A. E. Campbell. Athens: Ohio University Press, 2001.

———. *The President and His Powers*, 1916. In *The Collected Works of William Howard Taft*. Vol. 6, edited by W. Carey McWilliams and Frank X. Gerrity. Athens: Ohio University Press, 2003. Originally published as *Our Chief Magistrate and His Powers*.

Wolman, Paul. *Most Favored Nation: The Republican Revisionists and U.S. Tariff Policy*. Chapel Hill: University of North Carolina Press, 1992.

Acknowledgments

This book is nearly the final entry in the American Presidents series because, like William Howard Taft, I write best under tight deadlines. After receiving the assignment years ago, I procrastinated, in the Taftian spirit, until finally imposing a six-month deadline on myself and completing the manuscript with pleasure in a concentrated sprint.

I learned the creative satisfaction of writing short books on bracing deadlines from Paul Golob, the superb editorial director of the American Presidents series, who had played the role of kindly taskmaster and deadline enforcer when we worked together on a Supreme Court book a decade ago; working with him again was sheer delight. My friend Sean Wilentz, general editor of the series, completed this editorial dream team: learning from one of America's greatest historians and public intellectuals—who helped me better understand the differences between progressivism and populism and who resisted my Taftian efforts to reduce Theodore Roosevelt and Woodrow Wilson to the populist demagoguery they displayed in 1912—was a unique privilege.

I'm especially grateful to Lana Ulrich, in-house counsel at the National Constitution Center, where, in addition to her legal duties, she supervises the constitutional prep team. Lana's comprehensive, accurate, and detailed background memos helped me organize the primary sources into a condensed narrative, and her expert review of the footnotes and manuscript allowed us both to meet our deadlines. It's wonderful to have such a talented and engaged collaborator.

I was also fortunate to have a distinguished group of readers, whose comments and corrections greatly improved the manuscript and saved me from errors of fact and interpretation: Michael Gerhardt, Judge Douglas Ginsburg, George Liebmann, Jonathan Lurie, John Malcolm, Paula Marett, Hank Meijer, and Robert Post. Thanks to all of them for their intellectual generosity in sharing their time, insights, and deep knowledge of American constitutional law and history.

As I wrote this book, my beloved sons, Hugo and Sebastian Rosen, came into their own as enthusiastic readers. Their engagement with books is a joy to behold, and I learn so much from our debates and conversations. I'm so lucky that my adored parents, sister, and brother-in-law, Sidney and Estelle Rosen, Joanna Rosen, and Neal Katyal, offer love and wisdom every day.

I met my wife, Lauren Coyle Rosen, while beginning this book in January 2017. We fell in love at first sight and were engaged in June as the manuscript was completed. The wonder and gratitude I feel for her brilliance and creativity are ineffable. From her unrivaled ability to explain the most complicated philosophical concepts to her pathbreaking work in anthropology and law, she has inspired a mutual commitment to using our shared moments of leisure to cultivate our minds and spirits. It is a joy to learn with her every day and to bask in her radiant light. The six months devoted to writing this short volume will always have special meaning to both of us as the bookends to our blessed courtship.

Index

ABOUT THE AUTHOR

———

JEFFREY ROSEN is the author of five books, most recently *Louis D. Brandeis: American Prophet.* He is the president and CEO of the National Constitution Center, a law professor at George Washington University, and a contributing editor for *The Atlantic.* He was previously the legal affairs editor of *The New Republic* and a staff writer for *The New Yorker.*